Flecker of Dean Close

BY CHARLES WILLIAMS

THE REV. DR. W. H. FLECKER

Flecker *of* Dean Close

BY CHARLES WILLIAMS

the apocryphile press
BERKELEY, CA
www.apocryphile.org

apocryphile press
BERKELEY, CA

Apocryphile Press
1700 Shattuck Ave. #81
Berkeley, CA 94709
www.apocryphile.org

First published in London by the Canterbury Press, 1946.
Apocryphile Press Edition, 2011.

Printed in the United States of America.
ISBN 978-1-937002-19-0

PREFACE

For the information contained and for the papers used in this book, I am wholly indebted to Mrs. Flecker, as for the invitation to write it, and for the kindness she has shown throughout. The suggestion that it should be written was pressed on her by Old Decanians and by friends in Staines. The best introduction to it will probably be a note by an old pupil, Stephen Neill, then Bishop of Tinnevelly, which here follows:

" If Dr. Flecker had had greater advantages as a boy and a young man, he would have been among the foremost scholars of his age. He was a man of wonderful ability, of surprisingly wide erudition and knowledge.

" Mathematics and Divinity were his own special line of   y, but he was able to take the top classes in the school in Latin and French; and it is no exaggeration to say that if, at any moment, any master in the school was taken ill, Flecker was ready immediately to take the class for him, whatever the subject might be.

" He was a man of inexhaustible energy and a tireless worker, a voracious reader on many subjects, and could tear the heart out of a book very quickly. He managed for years to carry the whole burden of the administration of the school in addition to a much heavier programme of teaching than most Headmasters would venture to undertake.

" No one could know Flecker at all without appreciating the depth and simplicity of his religious faith. It was in the reading of the Scriptures that Flecker was at his best. He read in a manner all his own, with a far greater range and variety of tone than the ordinary reader. After more than twenty-five years I can recall the exact tones of his voice reading, ' Oh, earth, earth, earth, hear the word of the Lord ', and once as the concluding phrase of a lesson at dining-hall prayers, ' even as God also for Christ's sake hath forgiven you '. The ordinary boy found him formidable, but no one had any doubt that his main interest in life was the welfare of the boys committed to his care. Parents were often astonished at the extent and minuteness of his knowledge of their offspring, and he very rarely made a mistake.

" I discovered the kindness of his heart when I was in the Sanatorium and rather miserable. He came up quite late to ask how I was getting on; he then spoke in such tones of sympathy that I saw him in quite a new light.

" One of the deepest influences in Flecker's life was his home. He could not have done the tremendous work he did without the abiding refuge of a perfectly happy home life. It was a great wrench for him to leave the school after so many years as Headmaster; but with characteristic energy he set himself to make a new career in his old age. It was not in him to be idle. He learnt a new technique and built a completely new kind of life.

" He was fortunate in the setting of this work. There are few more beautiful things in England than the Thames Valley, and I know no church more attractively situated than St. Peter's.

" He went straight from his work to his rest; full of years and honours, and bearing a name which will last as long as Christian England lasts, as the creator of a public school inferior to many in numbers and in wealth, second to none in the affection it inspires in its children."

C. W.

FOREWORD

Dr. Flecker was in many ways a remarkable man. I am glad to be allowed to write a short Foreword to this account of his life and work. I knew him as Headmaster of Dean Close, a School founded to give boys an education based on Evangelical principles. He was an outstanding success in that position. The School to-day is largely, if not wholly, what he made it, and its position as a Public School has been won by virtue of what he gave to it. It has no claim to be entitled to any distinction except that it has given a definite but wide interpretation of its purpose. It was always possible that the purpose of its founders should be given a vague and narrow expression. It was due to Dr. Flecker that Dean Close did not fall into one of those errors. He struck exactly the right note with a firm touch which can be heard and appreciated to-day as much as it was a generation ago. Parents who cared very much for the influences to which their boys would be subjected and yet could not afford the high fees of the better known schools, learned to value what Dean Close had to offer, and boys came from all corners of England, and even Scotland, to take advantage of the rich provision made for a sound and sober expression on Church of England lines of the value of Christian education in the formation of character. His story is told in these pages and they must speak for themselves. All I wish to do is to commend this book to a wide circle of readers and that I do with all my heart.

CALDECOTE.

CONTENTS

								PAGE
	PREFACE	.	.	.	.	.	.	5
I.	UNDER VICTORIA	.	.	.	.	.	.	11
II.	THE TRAINING	.	.	.	.	.	.	15
III.	MARRIED LIFE	.	.	.	.	.	.	31
IV.	DEAN CLOSE	.	.	.	.	.	.	42
V.	THE FAMILY	.	.	.	.	.	.	58
VI.	THE WAY	.	.	.	.	.	.	69
VII.	STAINES	.	.	.	.	.	.	77

I

UNDER VICTORIA

WILLIAM HERMAN FLECKER was born on 10th December, 1859, at Roade, in Northamptonshire. He was the second of five children; and it is worth noting that his mother, Elizabeth Pardon, came of an old Huguenot family. The name Herman was given him from a barrister friend of his father's. His childhood was not of the easiest, the father was much away, the mother often in poor health. The family presently removed to Stratton, near Swindon, and Flecker and his younger brother had a long walk every day in order to reach the private school at Swindon which they attended. They often had to go home by way of the fields in order to take with them the milk from a farm.

He seems to have done extremely well at school. At his first he was particularly praised for arithmetic, history, and reading; at the age of twelve, he was said in his reports to be able to read " at times with thrilling power ". He was soon at the top of the school and his parents were recommended by the Headmaster to send him to some good public school " for we cannot teach him anything more ". He went for a short time to a boarding school at Clevedon, but this was closed owing to a bathing fatality, from the mental effects of which the Headmaster never recovered. The Fleckers moved to London soon after, and William was sent to Cowper Street School as a day boy; this school, when at a later date it had only a thousand boys, was thought to have declined considerably. Here he remained till he was sixteen, when he determined that he would now be independent and begin on a job of his own. He went one day into an agent's office and made application for one. It was in the year 1875.

It was 1875, in the second part of the Victorian age. It was a very great age, but this is not the place to enter into any detailed appreciation of it. One or two notes, however, must be made, because it is always desirable to understand something of the background against which any historical figure, small or great, moves. By 1875 the Victorian age, if we reckon from the accession of the Queen, had been in existence almost forty years; it was to last, if we reckon to the death of the Queen, not quite another thirty. To us—especially to those of us who were born in it—as we look back, it seems a time of peace and quiet. It did not, however, seem so to itself. It would be truer to say it seemed a time of last stands and last ditches, of desperate charges and forlorn hopes. The chances of foreign war were always felt to be high; the Queen's letters show how high they were—justly or unjustly—felt to be. But the distractions at home ran level with the outer danger. It was so, of course, in politics; but it is always so in politics; in every age, one way or another, the end of all things looms. The present writer has known men—and they by no means foolish—to whom the word " Liberal " meant the threat of death and destruction; he has known members of his family look startled at the word " Radical "; he has heard his father say that " Socialism is now everyone's bogy "; and he has observed " Bolshevism " take its place. He would not deny that " the end of all things " may at any time come. But the long verbal procession makes it seem less likely.

It was so then in politics, especially when the Women's Movement began, with its claims, agitations, defiances, and counter-defiances. It was so in religion. There had been in the previous century the Evangelical Revival, which had now settled; but then there had been in the nineteenth century the great return of dogma and the materialistic defiance of dogma. The danger of the High Church movement shook many; the present writer again has known an old lady who said to him: " I would rather see you dead than a Romanist ". (Peace be with her; she was, in fact, all but a saint.) Beyond England, Karl Marx defied the world with *Das Kapital* and the Vatican defied the world with the decree of Infallibility. Mr. Gladstone defied both, and most of England with him. And in 1876, Mr. Disraeli made the Queen Empress of India, after the great meeting; the same Disraeli who, in *Sybil*, had terribly revealed the world of the poor, and in *Coningsby*, the " Venetian Oligarchy " of the English aristocracy.

No; it was not a quiet age. Darwin and Huxley were quiet respectable gentlemen, but they added to the turmoil. It was not pretence—all that agitation. On the social side also, the Victorians were very well aware of the horrors of human existence, and they laboured to mitigate them. They were determined, in Johnson's great phrase, " to retard what we cannot repel, to palliate what we cannot cure ". There was a movement towards that palliation; it was less than it should have been, but it was there, and part of it was in the insistence on education. It is true that that age supposed (too rashly) that education and the good life were much the same thing. It was supposed—except indeed among Christians—that if a man were sufficiently well taught, he would see what was right and (naturally) do it. That error was not perhaps entirely overthrown until the present age, when we observed the whole energy of education directed to the inflicting of evil and inhuman deeds. But at least the Christians, of whatever Church or School, did not fall into that error—unless they were infected by " the spirit of the age ". They had heard of the Fall; they knew the need of Grace. Newman and Spurgeon, Manning and Tait, Westcott and William Booth, all declared that, on whatever else they disagreed. This indeed is one of the ever-present divisions between the world—however noble—and the Church—however foolish. It was a division which Flecker, and those who thought like him, thoroughly understood. Progress never so quickly, educate never so well, aim never so high at moral integrity or nobility of character; but unless that strange other thing, that hope beyond hope, and faith beyond belief, that distant exquisite certainty, were invoked, all was in vain. They felt it of the first importance, as indeed it is, to teach this to the young, while they were teaching them so much; for they thought that, without that, all education was likely to become perverted.

At first indeed, that view was widely held; as the century drew on, it became less common. The " respectability " of the Church began to disappear; that is to say, Christianity was no longer one of the necessary opinions of a gentleman. The defiances which the great champions on either side the division hurled at each other were less and less noticed by the mass in the middle. The wistful atheist and the reluctant Christian all began to disappear. But the champions continued the agelong battle.

A few dates sometimes make the changing state of affairs in any age clearer than discussion. In 1873, while Flecker was still at school, John Stuart Mill died—in the same year that Walter de la Mare was born; in 1874, G. K. Chesterton, Mr. Somerset Maugham and Gertrude Stein were born. In 1875, Charles Kingsley died; in 1880—the oddest coupling of all, and in a way the most significant—George Eliot died and Lytton Strachey was born. In 1881, Carlyle and Disraeli died; in 1882, Darwin and Rossetti, Pusey and Emerson. These names suggest the alteration. As great lay in a single historical fact; in 1871 the King of Prussia had been crowned German Emperor at Versailles. A new power had risen in Europe, which was to threaten all that had been, in all the conflicts of that age, thought to be just and compassionate and good.

II

THE TRAINING

IT was this society into which Flecker made his own personal entry when he was sixteen, that is, about 1875. He determined to become a teacher himself, and he managed to obtain, through a scholastic agency, a post in a private school at Stoke Newington. He took up the work at the age of seventeen, and remained for two years. His Headmaster, at the end of that time, wrote him a glowing testimonial, praising his tact, energy, and popularity; and if the story is true that in his first year he was sent out on the river in charge of seventy boys, it is clear that the Headmaster had some cause for gratitude. Even among the large classes and young teachers of those days, Flecker must have had a remarkable capacity, at seventeen, for direction and control.

It was in the same year that he first met Sarah Ducat, who was afterwards to marry him. She was at that time a student at the Royal Academy of Music, and the elder Flecker once took his son to the Ducats' house to hear Miss Ducat play Beethoven. He was young, tall, and bearded—beards then were a serious business, as the novels and (still more) the illustrations to the novels of the time show. The Miss Ducats, Sarah and her sister, looking down from above on the young man in the hall, were not impressed. When however, Flecker met them, he seems to have been immediately attracted by Sarah, and before the evening was over, to have known that he was in love. The girl was slower to return his affection, and her parents slower still to recognize it. At first they forbade the two to remain in touch. But they presently allowed a correspondence, and they afterwards yielded entirely. It was understood that when Flecker was twenty, they should be engaged.

It is odd now, looking back, to consider how finally fixed a thing marriage then generally was. Divorce was still, in 1879, unusual among the professional and middle classes, and still more unusual was the thought of it; that is, the interior preparation for it. Even Christians nowadays can hardly help being affected by their knowledge of it around them. They may repudiate the possibility; they may say, as the Church says, that divorce does not exist. But they must say so, in a sense, as a challenge. There was, then, no need of a challenge. One married; one was married. That was the fact. Those who said so were, of course, quite right. They entered on a way of life, to which (without any of the rhodomontade of a doubtful romanticism) they believed themselves to have been called. A husband or a wife might be a delight, but he or she was also a very serious and permanent duty. Understood so, it seems probable (on the evidence) that wife or husband often became a renewed and permanent delight.

The young Flecker had now a more intimate challenge than the seventy boys on the river—more intimate and perhaps more dangerous. The present writer owes originally to his own father the habit of quoting, about any lady so concerned, the text: ' Fair as the moon, clear as the sun, terrible as an army with banners", or " as an army in battle-array ". Militantly fair and clear, the beloved awaits our action. Something, in every sense, has to be done; and one of the more generally urgent things is to make some arrangement by which one may manage, more or less adequately, to support the beloved. Flecker had to make a career. While still at Stoke Newington he took a scholarship to Durham University. He determined to go there and read for a degree, and if possible, then to go on to a Fellowship that would take him through Oxford. He went.

Rather unfortunately, he read mathematics, for which he never really cared, but for which he had unusual ability. His mind was far more suited to history or to literature.

In a set of verses to his wife (printed in the *New College* (Eastbourne) *Magazine* July, 1881), he wrote:

> Nor can I indite
> In light fantastic numbers fancies fine
> With Donne or Quarles or Herbert.

The really interesting thing about this is that in 1881, Flecker could speak of Donne at that time with such casualness. Palgrave's *Golden Treasury*, first published in 1861, knows nothing of Donne, and very few young men of twenty-two at that time knew anything of Donne as a love-poet. Flecker apparently did. It may be added that this is one of those odd cases in which a whole general history of literary taste seems to be falsified. Without this unexpected example, we should never have supposed that a young Evangelical schoolmaster had read—even a bowdlerized—Donne. It is an interesting speculation what his judgment in literature would have been, had he become a critic. Thus, in a paper on the *Tempest*—at a time when its place in the Shakespearean Canon was doubtful, he wrote: " Everything seems to combine to consider it part of the latest work. The internal evidence is very strong."

But mathematics were more difficult to him. He had to work hard at them, and he allowed himself to be called to many other occupations. He was used as a singer and accompanist at concerts; he was asked to address all kinds of meetings; he was pressed to preach on Sundays in villages near to Durham.[1] He lost—anyhow, he lost from academic work—many hours given to long conversations with acquaintances and inquirers into religion. He was, if not a hot gospeller, at least always a missionary.

" A man ", he said, " has no right to be slovenly in the pulpit."

But the result of all this labour was to ruin his health. He often did not go to bed before midnight; he rose at

[1] He had a rich and resonant voice, and it is recorded that on one occasion he read and spoke with such conviction that a certain man in the congregation said: " I don't like to see so much confidence in so young a man".

four. Sometimes he never went to bed. He had little exercise, and he suffered from bad headaches. He felt profoundly his separation from Miss Ducat, and he experienced the sense of old age so often felt by the young—" that feeling of agedness which has made me forget that I am not yet of age. Still I am older than my years I feel—I want soon to get to the real earnest work of life."

He passed one examination in October, 1879. "I have come out first in this examination. The lists are just out. There are three exams which must be passed before a student can take a degree, this one which I have just passed is the second of the three." It was after this that he sat, at his father's instance, for an Oxford scholarship—" but I do not much want to get it. If I am to grind some years more at Mathematics, let it be at the proper place, Cambridge " (Jan., 1880). He wrote later from Oxford—" At last I am at Oxford, trying not with much success, to realize the true position of affairs. It all seems strange to me. It only needed that I should come to this old city, which for me has somehow or other, always had great fascinating powers; it only needed this to make me believe that I am in a great dream. I find there are a vast number of men in for the exam., and am beginning to wonder whether it would not be using the better part of valour for me to pack up and go to London by the night train . . ."

Later: "Here is a short and by no means exaggerated account of my torments. A mile's walk in the snow from quarter to nine till nine—nine to twelve a terrible struggle to get four hours' work done—failure and headache ensues—walk back in snow—swallow in wild haste an apology for dinner; walk back in snow—from two till five, try and do *five hours'* work, fail again—fearful headache, walk back in snow, make, or try to make myself agreeable to seven ladies—all this would surely drive me to do something desperate unless I had a safety valve of some sort—there are times when the cry 'who will show us any *good* thing? ' rises from the very depths of a man's soul with fearful force—I have no doubt that the cry arises from the consciousness of inability to show any good thing ourselves. . . . The paper this afternoon was simply horrible, and I came out of the exam. room angry with myself, for though the difficulty of the papers was certainly very great, yet I ought to have risen to the occasion—and I have not. However, it has taught me the great need of earnest and hard work for the next six months—at the end of that time I shall be in for my Durham Greats. I give myself this last chance—if I do not get a first class then I shall give up Mathematics for ever. I got hold of the life of Kingsley. . . . It is strange that all the men whom I admire, and indeed whom the whole world admires, are *not* mathematical, any of them. God alone knows what I am to do with my life. There are times when I feel a large store of energy in me and when I desire nothing better than to use it in His Service . . ."

He returned to Durham. There his real interests sometimes had a chance. Durham had at that time, two active and hostile parties of what were then called High and Low Church. The conflict was one of those great struggles which went on through the whole Victorian age. It is now clear to us that that conflict was itself, though a very real struggle, yet a sign of something greater—of the revival of dogma as dogma. It was this that was common to (say) both the Salvation Army and the Catholic Revival. It was this that Flecker's mind and heart seriously, if obscurely recognized. "I have set myself to reconcile the two great factions, Low and High Church, represented here in all bitterness, so that something unanimous may be done. At the same time I try to keep in the background as much as possible myself. I think for such an object I am justified in letting Mathematics go to the ground a little." But he did not let it go far. He wrote on another occasion: "My work is unfortunate; despite my long walk to-day I have a nasty headache; and have been trying to work in spite of it, thereby rendering it considerably worse. Our Senior man has just come in and wants me to take a Bible Class for him this afternoon. I have only three-quarters of an hour. I feel it my duty to go."

He generally did. The following extracts show him at this other work:

"On this Sunday I am to speak to the Waifs and Strays. I hope to speak from my heart to theirs. Poor things, they lead fearfully wretched lives: it seems almost a mockery to go from a well-spread table to speak to them of the Bread of Life, when they may be all the time hungry.

"I went with S. to the infirmary at Newcastle, and went through the wards with the doctors. But I could not bear to see the operations, though there were no *good cases* to-day I was told. It taught me such a lesson. I heard one man sobbing through pain: I can't describe the effect it had on me. I am sure of one thing, that I could not be a doctor unless I set myself to overcome very strong natural tendencies.

"A fortnight hence I am to open a debate in the Union Rooms. The subject is the opium question, and I shall strongly condemn our national position on the subject. Hot arguments will follow my paper. This horrid opium business is on my brain incessantly. The man who is to second me has been relying on me to furnish material for his speech, as well as my own—rather hard lines—so that my dreams have been opium-y.

"I am writing now with a man in my rooms who is waiting for me to read some Theology with him . . .

"I am trying very hard, though it costs me time and trouble, to set on foot some movement for the spiritual welfare, to use a hackneyed phrase, of the men here . . .

"There is a man up here who is fast ruining his health by riotous living. I was talking to him seriously the other day. Poor fellow! . . . I am awfully washed out, and a man is sitting in an armchair with no apparent intention of clearing out. . . . ' In the world ye shall have tribulation, but, be of good cheer, I have overcome the world ' can we not do all things through Christ? and if He has overcome, so may we. That verse seems to me eminently comforting to anyone who has to do a duty which is unpleasant.

or to suffer a trial hard to be borne. The Lord has sent a Comforter for us . . .

"I am very tired now—one of the students has asked me to give him music lessons! . . .

"Now just look how my time has gone since Sunday. Monday had to be at Newcastle. Tuesday write paper. Wednesday practice for Harvest Festival. Thursday choral meeting and debate and anthem at Cathedral— Friday I have been talking for about three hours to a man and have I am glad to say won him over . . .

"I have arranged for a little meeting to be held in my room on Wednesday nights. Just a few prayers and a short passage of Scripture, with a brief comment."

It was a rigour which seemed to him imposed on him by the whole scheme of things; he was not, he knew, free to neglect or avoid opportunities; he was, on the contrary, bound to make them. The whole of creation was an opportunity which had to be, at all times and in all places, localized. If we accuse those great and ardent souls of being over-serious, they answer simply that about the Crucifixion of our Lord and the possible damnation of our souls, it is quite impossible to be over-serious. It was their rational nature which drove them, as it has driven those of their kind through all the history of the Church. He wrote (8th Feb., 1880) to his fiancée: "One passage is to my mind a very solemn one, 'I am come a light into the world that whosoever believeth in me should not abide in darkness'. But how much we do abide in darkness; and though we often pray for more light, on the whole we are, many of us, at least very fairly content to grovel about jostled and hurt by all the things of this world as if we had never been provided with a 'lamp for our feet' so that we might walk surely and steadily. Then, too, the idea of those 'among the chief rulers' who, though believing, dared not confess, forces itself home to my conscience with power. You see it resolves itself into this, our finer faculties, the moral and spiritual, are not so keen as they ought to be, and would be if we used them constantly, while the lower perceptions are always in full working order; I mean that we approximate too much to an animal sort of existence, and so, when we are about to judge between two things of different natures, we are led to prefer that which is lower to that which is high; just the opposite to 'choosing rather to suffer affliction with the people of God than to enjoy the pleasures of sin for a season'. So again: 'Our ideas of God are not vivid enough; we think of Him in a sort of dream, just as we do of Charlemagne.'"

Yet Brother Ass, in the familiar phrase of St. Francis, refused to go on at this pace, spiritual duties notwithstanding, and in spite of all his rational sense of duty. Religion and love together could not save him from the threat of serious illness. The Oxford scholarship had not been gained. It was proposed he should try for one at Cambridge. He wrote: " I sometimes long for a year's rest. I think, nay am sure it would be the making of me, or at least the renovation of me. It is so many years since I could say 'Now, I will be quiet and rest'; when I have done least brainwork I have had most brain worry, and now I think at last I could calmly and quietly sever myself from Mathematics for a time—much as I (am supposed to) love them. This feeling I expect partly arises from the need of rest intruding itself so constantly upon me. I promised to say honestly if anything forces me to change my opinion as regards my ability to stand four years grind at Cambridge. Honestly no—only I think at least three months, if possible six months, I ought to put everything by and recruit; it is a long time since I have spent a whole week without work. I know, of course, that I should very possibly not be the *better* in health for my Cambridge grind, if I did it; but I can safely say that I don't think I should be much the worse. I worked off my headache to-day by a very fair day's work; but I find myself at the close, very tired. I had about half an hour's walk and enjoyed it thoroughly."

The Cambridge proposal was abandoned, and he concentrated on the B.A. at Durham, which he was proposing to take in June, 1880. Two quotations will show the effort he had to make and its result:

"I am so anxious to take my degree in June. I foresee a very busy vacation, and only hope I shall do as much work as I ought. It's not the slightest use for a man to imagine that he can pass a Durham exam. much more easily than an Oxford or Cambridge one; they are fearfully strict here."

"You will be sorry to hear that I cannot go through with my exam. I have knocked myself up so thoroughly that although I have done good papers, I am now utterly unfit for anything, and have in consequence, on the advice of the Dean, retired from the exam. I have tried to do an impossibility, and I think I almost succeeded; but for the last fortnight I have only had an average of two or three hours' sleep a day, and in consequence, I am beaten. It would be madness to lose a first which I can so easily get at Christmas. The consolation is that I have shown there is in me every capacity for the hardest work yet." (July 16th, 1880.)

All this while he had also been considerably weighed down by anxiety about Miss Ducat's own health. She had been ill, and had had to spend time with friends out of London, particularly with a family who lived near Swaffham in Norfolk. There Flecker went for his vacation also. He was in the habit, even when so near his fiancée, of writing short notes to her, which he pushed under the door of her room. It happens with others, but it does mean that the beloved is expected—fortunate if she can, as apparently Miss Ducat could—to read and to understand the confidences which the lover insists on offering. This is no criticism of him; it was a real and determined devotion. But such a devotion needs food on which to thrive. One does not go on confiding if the confidences fall into an unresponding heart or a slow intelligence.

The doctors insisted that Miss Ducat should live permanently out of London. The obvious solution, if it were possible, was for Flecker to find a job. An independent minister at Durham—himself only twenty-three—had been asking him " what I am going to do in life—I have been obliged to confess that I am further from knowing now than when I last saw him ". The independent minister probably meant more than an inquiry about Flecker's immediate step. In a general way, however, the high Omnipotence confines its direction precisely to the immediate next step, and does not always make that very clear. Flecker had retired from his Finals; he must either address himself to them again, or he must postpone them, do other work at the moment, and read for them presently. He determined on this second course; that at least might mean the possibility of marriage, and his wife and he might be able to nurse each other's health. They would certainly, in his view, be able to help each other towards God.

Education—that is, a post as a schoolmaster—was the obvious solution. He gave himself up to applications. He heard of a vacancy for a Vice-master at a school in Eastbourne, run by Mr. Fred Schreiner, who was the brother of Olive Schreiner, the writer, and William Schreiner, the South African statesman. He applied. His testimonials were returned, with a letter which explained that at his age—not yet twenty-one—he was too young to be trusted with the care of a hundred and fifty boarders and some authority over the junior masters. Flecker took the next train to Eastbourne, managed to obtain interviews, and returned with the appointment. It was a sign both of his resolution and of his power.

The school was known as the New College. When Flecker began work there in 1880 it was already a fairly successful establishment. His life there was busy and intense enough, but it had not about it the brooding crisis of Durham; the air was healthier; and he was clearly able to carry himself more lightly, without losing any of his serious intentions. He took part in the sports and the debates, edited the *New College Magazine* (in which appeared what is probably Olive Schreiner's first published story—*Dream Life and Real Life*), and started a Choral Society.

The immediate grimness of things passed a little. It was possible for him to write in one letter: " I often think of the old divine who for his nightly devotions simply said, looking up to Heaven, ' Thou knowest, Lord, we are where we were before '." This is that ease in Zion which Zion (truly desired) almost always brings, and without which perhaps the thorns and briars of the Parable may be supposed a little to have overgrown the Way.

A few other extracts from letters may be given here:

" I am often amused with the pranks of these youngsters. One needs the cuteness (real or imaginary) of twenty Yankees to be even with them. One fellow forcibly reminds me of the fat boy in Pickwick. I am certain he spends his school time asleep—and I have been trying to catch him once for all in the act. Do you know the traditional way? You go softly up, turn the boy's book over, retire, and call out ' So and so: are you working? ' He wakes up immediately and, of course, says 'Yes, Sir '. ' Well then, look at your book.' You may imagine his discomfiture at seeing only the covers. But it is, to my mind, a somewhat objectionable procedure, and I don't intend to put it into use.

" . . . Alternate Sundays, I am on duty. This means superintendence of all boys in schoolroom for half an hour before breakfast; for an hour in the afternoon (an awful hour) general supervision rest of time, Chapel duty, carving, and teaching for an hour and a quarter.

" . . . In a few moments I shall be carving, grinding away for sheer life at resisting legs of mutton, which will quite refuse to be cut into handsome slices.

" . . . I was very busy yesterday. Two choral meetings, an organ practice, and part of evening school to take. I am now trying to do two things at once; hearing a class say German verbs, and writing.

" It seems to me a Head Master, and an Under, too, has an awful responsibility on his shoulders; and in these days it is somewhat hard to know how to talk to boys, and what to say to them.

"I have promised to take a Bible reading with the boys. There is some weekly institution of the sort here, and I am not sorry to show how heartily I am in sympathy with that sort of thing, if properly managed.

". . . The first three chapters of Isaiah are appointed, but that of course is far too much, and I shall be content with the first. I know of nothing in the realm of poetry more beautiful than some of Isaiah.[1] When I have time I will sit down and mark extracts to form a connected reading to the boys at prayer time.

"Oh! the singing this morning! Had I energy enough I would attempt to describe it, but perhaps it is better to draw a veil over the scene. It harrowed me."

The Choral Society was inaugurated in November, 1880, and an account of the testing of voices appeared in the *New College Magazine*.

"For a long time" (says the Choral Report), "there will be a vivid impression, in one mind at least, of the Saturday afternoon which was set apart for trying the voices of those who wished to enter the Society. The Treasurer sat in state at the table in the reception-room; at the piano was seated the President. As the unfortunates, 'with bated breath', crept into the room and up to the piano, their names were solemnly entered on a list by the Treasurer. The question, 'Can you sing?' usually elicited a sometimes modest and generally truthful negative. Some of the renderings of well-known airs, such as 'God Save the Queen', were startling from their very originality. The repeated encouragements from the music stool to 'Open your mouth, like this', joined with the Treasurer's illustration of 'How it ought to be done', produced a variety of musical effect, from the awe-inspiring bass of Division I. to the shrill squeak of the youngsters."

For the Literary Society he read essays and took part in debates. His voice was noticed again. The *Magazine* said of a paper on the *Tempest*: "As a delight simply to the *ear*, it was a treat; the well-chosen words and the manner of reading them had the effect of the performance

[1] Milton took the same view.

of a piece of music." In politics, he belonged to the great Liberal tradition, of which we have almost lost the memory. In the following extracts from the records, the most notable thing is Flecker's support of the Oaths Bill—that which permitted Charles Bradlaugh (and any member of the House of Commons) to affirm his allegiance instead of swearing it "by Almighty God". The old accepted necessary Christian test was already ceasing; that men like Flecker, with a passionate belief at heart, could speak and vote against it, was perhaps the deciding thing. The great effort to unite Christianity and liberty (upon which we are now engaged) was beginning.

"Mr. Flecker first pointed out that the Treasurer's speech (the last speaker) was full of statements, both historical and political, which were totally unfounded, a thing not perhaps unusual in the orations from Conservative members. He (Mr. Flecker) thought the Boers had a sacred right to rise on behalf of their country, if, as he believed, it had been annexed against their wishes. The hon. gentlemen supported the Land Bill, because it was an honest and statesmanlike measure. No one, after reading the Bill and the speech which Mr. Gladstone delivered at its introduction, would ever charge him with half-heartedness and insincerity. He supported the Oaths Bill, because it was a step towards Disestablishment."

In December, 1880, he took his degree at Durham; it was a Second, so that the further Fellowship became impossible, and his purpose of a doctorate by the time he was thirty unlikely.[1] But his health had interfered with his work. He had written at one time: "I am sometimes very tired in Chapel, and don't stand up for the hymns. This was noticed, and a remark made to one of the under masters that I could not be very strong. He answered, 'No, for that time you preached more than three-quarters of an hour you nearly killed him.' I trust the poor man was not wounded much." And again: "I can't manage to get any work done for myself, however hard I try.

[1] He was, however, D.C.L. at twenty-nine.

I have come up to bed at ten o'clock quite fagged out. True, I spent a couple of hours to-day in writing something which I trust I shall *not* be fool enough to put in the Mag. But what can I do?—tired at night, tired more in the morning. I am determined to conquer it. Went for an hour's walk to-day, and felt the air quite oppressive." And of his original aim, the doctorate: " The old ambition has gone—died—nor do I mourn it; for it was a low-lived thing; it is nothing to me now. That I should be glad to have some money, I confess. I often think that were any good post to offer itself in the Colonies, I would go."

The ambition might seem low-lived; what was certainly long-lived was his determination to be able to marry and (so far as he could), provide Miss Ducat with a home and happier health. He took firm steps towards this with a business-like clarity worthy of the greatest Romantic lovers; to whose company indeed, in his own degree, and after his own style, he seems to have belonged. It is to be admitted that he would probably have hesitated over the attribution. One must not press the reference to Donne; yet the great lines of Donne.

> Here the admiring her my mind did whet
> To seek thee, God—

are not alien from him or many lovers like him. " A new smell", as George Fox said after his conversion, "had gone up from the earth." It was his business, in religion, in love, in his vocation, to follow it. It was the movement in his words of " the God of Israel, and the Cross of his Son ".

He went to see Mr. Schreiner. The Headmaster hinted at his younger colleague's success, and even hinted farther, at the possibility of a future partnership. " Ay, sir, but ' while the grass grows '—the proverb is something musty." Flecker, as a resident Vice-master, was then at a salary of £150. He needed a non-resident post at a higher salary. The Headmaster hesitated, temporised, and gave way. He agreed to the non-residency; he promised a salary of £175, to be raised in the next year, if all went well, to £200. He made arrangements for private pupils. And he began to prepare also for the expenses of the marriage. The following extracts record his activity:

"I have had a few more words with Schreiner, and have been very frank with him about the matter. He thinks I shall not be able to get here to morning school before breakfast: I say 'I shall', but I cannot deny that I shall not be quite so useful to him, and it does seem cheek to ask more screw for being less useful. I told him at last, that at the worst, I would marry, and still be resident, but that I would much rather not."

"The difference between £175 and £200 is only £8 for one Term. I shall make *more* than that amount this Term by private coaching. I shall have £75 in hand *quite* at the end of Term. I want you to tell me if your people think £175 enough—I would almost ask you to telegraph. The necessity of making money is so obvious."

"I called in on the father of the fellow whom I am coaching for the First B.A. and I heard good news. His son will continue with me to July twelve month, so I am certain of £12 from him this Term. Then there is another three guineas I am sure of for next Term, so that I am half-way on already to the £30 which I want to make. Supposing I spent *nothing* between this (May) and August 10th, I should have £80. Reckoning our expenses as on an average £4 a week, and throwing in £10 extra for the marriage itself, there is still left a clear £40 to begin the New Year with. It will be my aim to make it £50. Have I understated our expenses?"

The parents on both sides were at first reluctant to consent. The elder Flecker was disappointed that his son had given up the idea of Cambridge; and both he and his wife thought that the early marriage might interfere with their son's career. The father seems to have threatened to stop the marriage; the son replied by saying that he was old enough to manage his own affairs: "If I have to go to the Cape of Good Hope I will, or anywhere to take me out of the way for three or four years." His mother wrote to recant and to soothe, though regretfully. Flecker wrote to Miss Ducat: " She seems to coincide with the view that we are doing a foolish thing; as if I ever pretended or wanted to be worldly wise; but she reminds me, and with justice, that my father's pet dreams as to my future are utterly knocked on the head, and that after all he is somewhat to be pitied just now. I am rather pleased for many reasons, that we are going to marry on such a small income. Father complains that he has allowed me latitude to a too great extent."

Her parents had also, though also with reluctance, assented. The marriage was arranged for the Bank Holiday, 1st August, 1881. There was then another week of term to be gone through. The Headmaster asked what arrangements Flecker was making about it. Flecker said he would be back as usual on the day after the wedding. The Headmaster laughed, and said " Rubbish! " But he was at early morning school the next morning. The marriage was to begin with work: " I am reckoning on spending a honeymoon of real hard work; five hours a day at least. It must not be merely a talk about it, but a *fait accompli* if I am to take my London degree in October, and upon that I have set my heart." He spent the Sunday afternoon of July 31st putting his books in order in the furnished rooms which they were to occupy in the Old Town, opposite the church. During the afternoon he heard the church bells ringing a peal, and found " that it was in honour of the home-coming of Squire Gilbert and his bride, who live at the Manor House close to us. It was very nice to hear them, and the only sensible word the landlady let fall from her tongue was to say that it was ' quite appropriate for you, Sir '. I sat down and rested in the course of my labours, and prayed the first prayer which I have uttered in our home." It must have been at the same time that he wrote on a white slate the words: " As for me and my house, we will serve the Lord. May God bless my darling wife, now and forever. W.H.F." The next day, after the wedding, he brought his wife home, and took her to a table where the slate with its dedication lay. Slate and dedication, after more than sixty years, still exist.

III

MARRIED LIFE

Two months before the marriage, Flecker had written to Miss Ducat: "I *do* fear that you will find married life rather wearisome. You know they say that 'no man is a hero to his valet', and it is equally true that few men are heroes to their wives, and I shall not be one of the few. I am a very *very* ordinary man." He is an unwise bridegroom who thinks anything else, subject always to that high and infinite charity which a wife, in some extraordinary way, seems so often able merely to diffuse round him. No man can possibly judge whether the masculine, as such, is as generous as the feminine. I do not say the male and the female; that grosser and less adequate distinction does not altogether correspond to the more delicate distinction. We are perhaps, nevertheless, obscurely right in generally attributing rational judgment to the masculine and irrational generosity to the feminine. In marriage certainly the feminine is capable of both. Few married men have not been astonished at the extreme accuracy of judgment and the extreme generosity of temper displayed by their wives.

The serious beginnings of that state are apt to be equally beautiful and equally difficult under whatever high symbol of religion or in whatever intensity of purpose they may be displayed. "As for me and my house, we will serve the Lord." So; but Flecker did not leave on record (and it was not for the present writer to ask Mrs. Flecker), the thousand adjustments which that service involved. All those adjustments are part of that service. The glory of God is in facts; and those devoted to the glory have to deal with facts. It is perhaps true that the present age has a greater sense of *all* the facts; it is certainly true that it has a less vivid sense of the glory. The odd—and shattering—fact about the great Evangelical tradition is that it was determined to repose on nothing but the glory. Nor certainly did the other—call it Catholic—tradition do otherwise. They disagreed; they disputed; as Flecker at Durham had found them disagreeing and disputing. That was partly ignorance; we understand now, more of what lay behind the two great Ways. But as Flecker had tried at Durham to bring them together, so all his life. He would not (most properly) ever compromise on doctrine. But short of that, he desired very greatly, as far as he could understand and crave it, the peace of the Church.

The peace of his household; the peace of the Church—a peace to be achieved by industry, patience, and devotion. He gave his own to that double peace. His vocation lay in the instruction of the young. His private business was to fit himself for, and give himself up to, that; at the same time that, with his wife's energy and intelligence and charity to nourish him, he provided, as far as he could, for her needs and his own. It is done, as we all know, by money. " Money is a medium of exchange "—of heavenly exchange as well as worldly. Flecker accepted the—for most men—inevitable condition, and set to work to make the necessary money. For, then as now, it had—quite definitely—to be made.

The discipline of the household—a joyous discipline—was simple. They rose at five or five-thirty, ate some fruit, went for a short walk, and then Flecker did some of his private work. He went off to morning school at half-past seven, and breakfast followed. After which, the day's work began. This involved not only the normal routine of the school, but arrangements for private lessons. There were visitors to Eastbourne who were willing and able to pay for private coaching for their sons, as well as settled residents. Enough funds were gathered together from these various sources, to make it possible for them to move (since their rooms were not satisfactory), and to take and partly furnish a large house. It was not far from the school. An arrangement had been made by which Flecker's two younger sisters were to live with them—the house had nine bedrooms—and Mrs. Flecker was to coach them for Music and the Senior Cambridge Local. But when this arrangement came to an end—it had turned out admirably and the two girls passed their various examinations—they took a smaller house and, afterwards, went again into rooms. The reason for this last decision was simple. It was that they had not so much money. Flecker gave up a good deal of his work at the school. He had determined to be ordained, when old enough. He had therefore, to study that "queen of the sciences", divine theology. We have heard, often enough, of the young creatures of the Middle Ages, at twelve years old or younger, reading that lordliest of all contemplations in the candle-lit cold of morning at the Universities. Flecker was older; he was a son of the Victorian age; he was living in rooms at a seaside town. The theology, it must be admitted, was in many points different. But the great principle was not different. It was the passionate desire of the serious heart to understand, define, and proclaim, "the ways of God with man".

He had to take a Cambridge Examination in Theology. Mrs. Flecker was as devoted to the purpose as her husband. She assented to, and encouraged the move into rooms. She took a post as daily governess to a young girl. She came to an agreement with her husband that they should keep absolute silence at home, so that he should be able, continually, to concentrate his mind on his coming examination. Conversation therefore, was limited to the morning walk to her house of employment. It was a very remarkable effort and (as so often happens) when it was well begun, a still greater effort had to be made. The landlady wanted twice as much rent; the summer season was approaching, and she would not—perhaps she could not afford to—be satisfied with anything less. But the Fleckers could not afford to pay it. They had therefore to leave. For the time they were given shelter by friends, and Mrs. Flecker took on herself the additional business of searching for somewhere to live. She eventually found a small unfurnished house in a row of new villas; some of its rooms were yet unfloored, and the walls were only just being plastered. Their belongings were stacked in one room; they moved in.

After all this effort, it was more than satisfying that Flecker passed the examination; he was indeed first on the list in two subjects—the Old Testament and the Book of Common Prayer. He had secured a title at an Eastbourne church—St. John's Meads, and on 19th May, 1883, he was ordained by Dr. Durnford, then Bishop of Chichester. He was twenty-three years old.

St. John's Meads at that time was not, in some respects, an easy church to serve. The Fleckers' home was a long way from the church, and it became impossible to return after the morning service. They therefore fell into the habit of taking sandwiches with them, and eating them in the vestry, where Flecker finished preparing his evening sermon. One of the congregation, a gardener employed by General Holroyd, sometime Governor of Assam, found this out and invited them to use his own home in a lodge near by. General Holroyd in turn, discovered this, and insisted that they should lunch and spend the day with him.

The church itself had one inconvenience. It was small and stood among trees. Any storm of wind, near the coast as it was, resulted in bringing down twigs and small boughs on to the roof, so that even Flecker's admirable voice was completely unheard, and the small choir of little girls sang in vain against it. The parish work, for other reasons, was almost as difficult. Flecker all his life, had a great idea of his duty to his congregation; he approved of careful visiting, and (both here and at Staines later), seriously practised it. But the parish was scattered; and many belonged to it who would come for special reasons—as for marriage or to have children baptized—or occasionally, who would not or could not attend regularly. Such, for example, were the Beachy Head Coastguards. Visiting had been neglected, and (in many cases) was not wanted.

There is a story that Flecker once went to visit some remote cottages on the side of the cliff. He knocked and knocked at one door; for long, no answer. Then from a window above a woman's voice asked his business. He explained. The voice said: " Well, we've done without the likes of you for years, and we'll go on doing without."

Socially, the Fleckers did better. Olive Schreiner came often, bringing flowers (" she had always an air of great sadness "). They mixed with other residents; they went to musical evenings, then a common social amusement. They prepared for their next advance.

The City of London College School was on the point of opening, and Flecker applied for and obtained the post of Headmaster. He was twenty-four. An old friend, writing to congratulate him, said: " You have that dynamic force —it is called so—in common with Jowett and all good generals, and good schoolmasters—which enables you to teach with authority. Again I reckon you to have that flexibility, or versatility, on which Matthew Arnold discoursed to the Eton Boys—that enables you to manage boys, somewhat; but it is more important in its functions as you exercise it in managing adults, and directing your affairs. What is generally expected of you, you will do well. You have a ready, pleasant manner with people, with no shyness nor much intolerance of the ordinary dullness."

He had something more. No doubt, as great masters have taught us, " all luck is good ", and no doubt Flecker would have sincerely believed that what is usually called " bad luck " could have been the means of good. It is certain that (outside sin) the position in which at any moment we find ourselves is precisely the best for us at that moment. But what the world calls " good luck " has its advantages. Others have worked as hard, and believed as strongly, as Flecker, and (humanly speaking) failed. Less may be asked of them; with every step upward, the Judgment becomes stricter. This at least must be meant by the Dominical saying: "Woe unto you when men shall speak well of you." Yet our talents are not to be left idle. It is a narrow way; but our Lord promised nothing else.

At any rate, a certain "good luck" now began to accompany the Fleckers. Mrs. Flecker was expecting her first child, and at such times all money is welcome. The Vicar of Holy Trinity, Lee, was in need of a curate, and happened to be in Eastbourne. On the strength of general report, he had an interview with Flecker, and offered him the post—at twice the expected salary. The Bishop specially arranged for his ordination to the holy order of priesthood before he left Eastbourne. Priest and Master of Arts, headmaster and curate, he went on to pursue the Glory of God in London. It was August, 1884.[1]

Their welcome was more than friendly. It became a rare thing for the two to have an evening to themselves. The men of the congregation at Lee used to come round in small groups to the house, often bringing their wives. The house was in Gilmore Road, Lewisham, and the new Headmaster went up every morning to the school in Moorfields. But the most important thing, once Flecker's success in both his posts was reasonably certain, was the near birth of the child. It happened on 5th November, 1884—a day of quite dense fog. It was a son; he was baptized Herman Elroy Flecker; presently, at Oxford, he changed his first name because of its foreign sound, and became James Elroy Flecker. His mother told Miss Geraldine Hodgson, his biographer, that soon after he was born, "he had the appearance of a child of two months, with well-developed and already expressive features. His blue-grey eyes, his sudden movements, and (more than all) his masses of long black hair, gave him an elf-like look." A remarkable number of gifts were sent in by friends and members of the congregation.

The next year, Flecker, pressed by friends, made his first journey to Europe. He was never, in any wide sense of the word, a European, and it was rather the scenery of Europe than Europe of which he wrote. In 1885, the

[1] During the early days at Dean Close, he went back to his old habits of working till the early hours of the morning in order to become first B.C.L. and then D.C.L. In order to write his thesis for this he had to use certain law books written in technical German which the native German masters could not translate for him. Flecker mastered them himself.

separation between Europe and England was greater than it is to-day, and that not only because of the great and fatal year during which England, beyond any expectation or wish of her own, became Europe in arms. Uninstructed and ignorant, the English alone then defended the " two thousand years' tradition of civility " which began when the Persian armies fell back from Greece into Asia. But besides that high chance, many things have altered since 1885; scholarship and even (to an extent) tolerance. Not that Flecker was intolerant; he was not. But he hardly then spoke the language of Europe or Europe his. He took (to help with expenses) the chaplaincy of Ragatz, and went on expeditions. Mrs. Flecker went to the Isle of Wight with the baby to stay with friends. It was nearly twenty years before he was able to take her also to Switzerland and Italy. " It was ", she has said, " their real honeymoon." The following extracts are from his letters home:

" We mounted along the valley of the Rhine, until we came to three houses and a church. We had a glass of milk and I asked to see the church. There was no floor, save the ground—mother earth itself—the turf just scraped off and benches (very, very rough) put on instead. It is a Protestant Church, and one service per annum is held there, on Ascension Day. Then we went on and clomb and clomb till we came to a tiny village. Four heads of families—miles away from the world—very close to heaven—such a view as I shall never see again, for by this time the clouds had gathered thick on the right, and there the hills and dark fir trees looked black and frowning. On the left the sun was shining on lovely green slopes and purple heights—below us the rain was sparkling down from white clouds. It was perfectly beautiful. Every green, and purple and yellow you have ever seen and admired, was there spread at our feet. And then we turned to come down, finished our journey in five and a quarter hours, and in a pouring rain."

" The Cathedral at Chur is the most interesting Cathedral I have ever seen. Old MSS. dating back to 784, and with the very seal of Charlemagne—and paintings and wood carvings, and jewelled cups—and an interesting sacristan."

"*Ragatz*, 1885. Have come into Switzerland again from Bellagio. We are half way up the Maloya Pass. We had to get out of our carriage and walk the last eight miles, but that is a bagatelle. I don't notice the least fatigue. I go on to Ragatz from San Moritz by *diligence*. All these hotels are very fine. The one at Bellagio especially. They do everything for you. I believe if I were to put my head out on the mat at night, I should find it there clean shaved in the morning. I don't know about the mountains inspiring one to noble words. They are very grand and still, and noble themselves—and one feels more inclined to be quiet than to speak much about them, or in their presence. The memory of them will remain as something good to have. Owing to the rain I am stopping at Maloya over night—going on to Ragatz tomorrow morning. We are now at the entrance of the Engadine. This hotel is quite new, and is a marvel to behold. Built here, far away from town or village, thousands of feet above the sea, it contains every luxury. Marble staircases—Turkey carpets—pianos and billiard rooms—daily concerts, a grand assembly room, with polished floors, capable of seating 2,000 people. Four hundred people can sleep here. I sat up fairly late, relying on being called at four-thirty this morning. What was my dismay, when Boots woke me at five-sixteen!—saying in frightened German, that he had overslept, and that I had only nine minutes to dress and catch the *diligence* which waits for no man. Well I did it! You can imagine what was the quality of my washing and dressing! I remembered to put on warm clothes, and thankful I am that I did so, for I had a very cold drive, and did not get to Ragatz until dusk. I must make some arrangements about the sermons tomorrow."

"I can look back on the past four years, and thank God for them. We will pray that the future may be free from anything that should mar our life together, or with God. Much doubt in choosing Sunday morning's sermon. Indeed, I spent more than two hours in finding it."

" 'Henceforth, my brethren, be strong in the Lord, and in the power of His might'."

" In the afternoon I am going to preach on ' I will hear what the Lord God will say concerning me '."

" M. comes up and asks me to talk. He was at church this morning. I doubt whether he has been before for many a long day. He seems to have been touched. I prayed, even as I preached, that he might be, and I chose ' The Kingdom of Heaven ' for that purpose. I should indeed be thankful if he could see his way clearer. I have talked very earnestly, but very humbly, for a whole hour with him. I could only get out of him that I put the matter very clearly. I can see that he is troubled a great deal."

" I look upon my ride of yesterday as having given me the best view I have had of the snow and ice mountains. The sun rose above them beautifully. One can imagine that if the Lord were to come again for the FINAL TIME, the clouds might lift, and show HIM standing upon those glorious, never trodden, white peaks. I grieve at this craze of ascending these lovely heights."

" *Davos, September 18th*, 1885. One of the grandest expeditions I have had—Ballance and I went by ourselves. We started off in an *einspanner*, with a guide, at seven a.m.— drove through the Fluella Pass for three and a half hours, until we reached the highest point of the Pass, where is a little inn, called the Hospice. Here we set out on foot, clambering up above the stream—above the grass, above the daisies, above the very snow itself, until we came to the top of the Schwarz Horn, where is a heap of stones and a cross. There is much more snow about than there has been for many years. The sky was lovely. The view perfect. One piece of mountain will for ever remain in my memory, Pitz Bernina and the Morter Aitsch and Roseeg Glacier—lovely pure white high up into the clouds. We saw the Tyrol Mountains in the East—the Bernese Oberland, with all its great peaks, in the West. But nothing was at all equal to the Pitz Bernina."

" We have had a faultless week to end up with. On the Schwarz Horn we had to cross a very large and fine glacier, like a pure white giantess. Our guide was a very interesting old chap—sixty-seven years old—who has been up and down the Horn since he was sixteen. It is over ten thousand feet high. I have done my first mountain very happily and successfully, and had an unequalled view, yet as I turned my back on the Schwarz Horn, I remembered with a thrill of joy that it was my first step homewards."

He returned to a great change, the change that was to settle his life for thirty-seven years. The Governors of the City of London College School had determined to move it from London to Catford. It had developed satisfactorily enough under Flecker's direction, but there was a general feeling (in which he did not share) that it would do better still if it were moved. He determined to resign. The Governors were unwilling; it seems that the boys were still more unwilling. Some fifteen (out of about sixty) suggested that they might become boarders at his house at Lewisham. The actual house was too small, but there was at first an idea that, with another house, the plan might be possible. It became clear, however, that it would not do permanently, and he began to look for another job.

It was at this time that, away in Cheltenham, the Evangelical party in the Church determined to establish a school as a memorial to one of their number, Dean Close, who had been the Rector in the eighteen-twenties. It was to be a Public School which was to be based on Evangelical principles. By 1885 the growth of the High Church party in the Church of England was marked. This school was to be a centre of the other tradition. Flecker heard of it, and heard that a Headmaster was needed. It was exactly what he desired. It would give opportunity for all his serious capacities and all his real devotion. He applied. He asked the Council of his old school for testimonials. Some of them were High Church, but, High Church or not, they were all agreed on what they could say. They praised his industry, his ability, his character. He was invited to Cheltenham for an interview.

On the evening before he was to go, a number of

members of his Lee congregation came to his house after evening service, and implored him not to leave. They offered to collect money, to take a house, to send their sons to his school, to guarantee an income. The strength of this appeal was so intense and sincere that he was shaken. It was almost midnight when he gave way and agreed. They left; and they had hardly gone when he cried out to his wife: "No, I was wrong. A man should not be dependent on his friends." It had not, certainly, been only their friendship which had won him; but also the sense of the duty he might be thought to owe them. Yet it might have been unsatisfactory; these arrangements, even among the twice-born, are apt to be unreliable, especially after some years. He wrote that same night to each of his visitors, explaining his views and offering his apologies. In the morning he started for Cheltenham, and was unanimously appointed. The School was to be opened in May, 1886.

The two left Lee amid the same display of affection that had welcomed them. Two maids from the congregation wished to go with them, one as cook and one as nurse. Other members helped in the packing; one friend even went down with them, taking a hamper of food and necessaries for the first day or two. There was a presentation of a parting gift of £120. Of the letters sent him, thanking him both for his public and private help, and—what is in the end the only important thing—for his manner of life, it is sufficient to quote two:

"He little knows what good his daily life has been to me." "That precious sermon has been much on my mind, and the last fortnight the desire to write and thank you has quite haunted me." The sermon was on Psalm xvii, 15: "As for me, I will behold thy face in righteousness: I shall be satisfied, when I awake, with thy likeness."

IV

DEAN CLOSE

THE verse from the Psalms with which the last chapter ended might stand as a motto for this chapter. But if it did, it would indicate not only the duty of a Headmaster of Flecker's type towards his pupils, but also the difficulty of it. How does one impose and evoke righteousness upon and in the young? How does one, in the slightest degree, suggest to them that their satisfaction may be in the Divine likeness? How—without making them unnatural? How—without making them prigs, and worse than prigs? Or without, as is so easily done, frightening them wholly away from any thought of it?

In 1886, the problem was both less and more than it is to-day. Then many of the boys came from what were called—and quite frequently were—" Christian homes ". That kind of home, with all its advantages and disadvantages, is now rare. Even Christian homes to-day are likely to be unlike the Christian homes of that period, and as the Evangelical tradition has in many ways relaxed or faded, the unlikeness has grown greater. The strength and weakness of that august tradition was that it so often implied, if it did not demand, the equivalent of a mystical experience. This, at least, had been its fundamental in many of its manifestations, from the Apostolic beginnings of the Church to the Evangelical revival of the eighteenth century. But the things of which St. Paul wrote with passion to his converts cannot be demanded—of heaven or of the young. Even such a man as John Wesley had tended to overwatch too carefully the spiritual life of the all-but-babes of Kingsmill School.

Since the Church (according to the wisdom of its Lord) was permitted to become an institution, it has been true that the institutional side has had to be preserved. The promise that the gates of hell should not prevail against it has applied—if only just—to that institutional side. It has been the labours of great saints and confessors which (under the Grace) have still preserved it. Many of them are known; many more are not. The Victorian age in England had its full number; so, doubtless, has our own. Not the least among them were those whose vocation was to be teachers of men, and of these, not the least those who were to be teachers of boys. Arnold of Rugby, Thring of Uppingham, Flecker of Dean Close, were concerned to produce " Christian gentlemen ". The phrase has been mocked till it has lost meaning. Yet both parts of the phrase had, and ought to retain, a great meaning. They carried on, together, the far vision of the union of faith and humanism, of the supernatural and the natural,—say, of God and Man. They preserved the tradition of Style. A Christian gentleman was one who, in the words of the Old Testament, loved justice and walked humbly with his God; in the words of the New, who loved God and his neighbour, and who carried himself therefore with devotion to the one and with charity to the other. *Caritas*, and again *caritas*.

It seems that Flecker himself had not (in a sense, fortunately) passed through any personal mystical experience; he had not been, in that particular sense, " converted ". He was preserved therefore from demanding from the young, any emotional crisis; he was saved from these excesses which have occasionally ruined the Evangelical tradition. It is nothing against the tradition; it is, perhaps, something against some of its preachers. Dean Close was free from it. On the other hand, his own very real piety and faith preserved him from sterility, in his soul and in his work. The present writer would not too rashly accept the testimony of his " old boys ". Cool and correct judgment about one's own past is always difficult; one is apt to be lured into thinking that it was better or worse than it was, that one's teachers were much more or much less effective than they were, and it is no more proper excessively to praise than excessively to blame. But it is, in a sense, more handsome. There is, however, a point at which reasonable caution becomes foolish incredulity, and it is impossible to read the many letters which were written about Flecker's career at Dean Close without recognizing that they were written not only in good faith (which is much) but in common intelligence (which is quite as much in these matters); that they speak the truth not only as their writers see it now, but as in all human probability it was then; that Flecker meant this to them, and even more than this, and that his reign at Dean Close profited others to a much greater and longer effect than his modesty would have supposed.

The school was opened in May, 1886. There was a lunch to the Committee, the staff, visitors, and the boys. The number of the boys was twelve—nine boarders (of whom seven came from the City of London College School) and three day-boys. The parents and guests were mostly strangers to each other, and the method of arranging the lunch was for one of the members of the Committee to stand on a chair and call out the names of a lady and of a gentleman. They came forward, were formally introduced, and went to their seats. But they were not always aware of their neighbours. One lady close to Mrs. Flecker began to talk of the new Headmaster, commenting on and criticizing his youth. She was suppressed, though all such criticisms could not be, and were indeed often quite innocently offered. Two old ladies of the neighbourhood, visiting Mrs. Flecker, at that time, said to her seriously: " It's rather a dreadful thought that immortal souls should be in the care of such young people as you are." There was, however, an advantage in it which they could hardly see. Flecker neither expected from his charges the experiences of age, nor did he wish to deny them the experiences of youth—of which secular education is one. But there were also more extreme opponents. At a certain dinner, a master from Cheltenham College took Mrs. Flecker in to dinner. He chatted to her about the schools, and ventured to ask why another school should be started in a town already well-supplied. She advanced, timidly, a remark on its Evangelical character. "Oh Evangelicalism!" he exclaimed, "that's as dead as a doornail."

There were, however, more immediately serious difficulties than such elderly doubt or juvenile contempt. There was, first of all, the business of clearing the grounds. The soil was heavy, and the garden and field belonging to the school were then only ploughed land. Mrs. Flecker, injudiciously venturing on it one morning, lost both her shoes before she could get away. The weeds were reduced, and potatoes planted, but the weeds (symbolically!) almost overcame the potatoes. However, the ground was conquered at last; the garden was turned into a garden; and vegetables removed to the adjoining field. An orchard of trees, given by the Headmaster, was planted, and the rest sown with grass. Eventually games were possible there. It was afterwards decided to build the chapel on one of the fields near the other school buildings.

While this was going on outside the buildings, disaster occurred inside. In the second or third term, the ceilings began to crash. That of the Headmaster's study fell one day when he had just risen from the table; the small James Elroy had just run across the landing one morning from his bedroom to his mother's when the ceiling above it, and that of the hall below also fell. The Headmaster decided at once that the boys—forty or more—must not be left in such peril in their dormitories. They must go to another house. All the bedsteads and all the bedding, all clothes and linen, had to be got across—it was a Saturday—before the Sunday. And as soon as possible all the ceilings were taken down and replaced. There were opportunities—and some were taken—for jests in the Cheltenham papers, though indeed the fruit of such jests lay rather in the new and strong replacements which were substituted for the old. It has been remarked, on other occasions, that so often the opponents of the Faith prefer not to press the jest too far. Christendom can absorb very much, and humour and irony are among its lesser conquests.

Numbers began to rise from the first. The school had originally been designed and built to house fifty boys. It opened with twelve. At the opening of the second term the number had risen to forty, and applications were still coming in. It was decided to begin more building at once, on a basis of accommodation for two hundred and fifty boarders. Presently it became necessary, even so, to exclude day-boys. A suggestion was made that the number should be raised to three hundred, but this Dr. Flecker refused. He believed it to be a Headmaster's duty to know and have in mind each of his boys individually, and though he had allowed the number to rise to two hundred and fifty, he was firm against more. It seems indeed astonishing that he could have managed to do as much as he did with even the smaller number. But that he did, the letters and records of the old boys themselves seem to show. He introduced into the school what was then a " new system ", by which boys did not remain in the same class for every subject, of whatever standard in any subject they might be. " We were in whatever class our knowledge of the subject qualified us for." This of course does mean individual attention and may at least help individual growth. At one time the House system was tried. Two houses on the other side of a large field rented by the school were taken, and two married masters put in charge. Neither came up to his wishes. Health and discipline began to go down. Eventually the masters resigned and Dr. Flecker, with considerable relief, re-assumed full control. It is indeed always a difficult thing to delegate powers; more especially when one is held finally responsible—both by others and by oneself—for physical health, intellectual development, and spiritual knowledge.

Spiritual knowledge—and by that is meant, quite literally, spiritual knowledge—was indeed one of the aims he set before himself. He had, of course, on his side the atmosphere of many of the homes from which the boys came to a degree which it is now difficult for us to appreciate. Many were sent because coaching, food, and health were carefully attended to; even the cleanliness was rare for a boys' school then. But many were the sons of the Evangelical clergy; most came from Christian families. (It may be admitted at once that there are two sides to this; a Christian atmosphere in the home has as often revolted as it has attracted the young. This is not to say so much against such a Christian atmosphere as is sometimes thought. The revival of Christianity is likely to be assisted for a time by the atmosphere of atheistical homes. The home is a very great thing, but it often has a centrifugal as well as a centripetal influence, and the centripetal often does not get to work until the centrifugal has had its fling.) But a school is not a home, and no amount of kindness or care will make it so. The declaration of the Doctrine is in danger of becoming a subject. It is this subject which has to be related to the most hidden longings, the most delicate emotions, the crudest faults, of two hundred and fifty individual boys.

" 'The proper study of mankind,' " Flecker once wrote in a letter, " is (with all due deference to Mr. Pope) not man but God." He was, of course, right. But for a schoolmaster and a Headmaster, the difficulty lies precisely in the word "study".

There are, in general, two methods by which that study can be made real—the public statement and the private. Flecker, as every man occupying such a position must, used both; the difference between him and many men occupying such a position was that he seems to have been good at both. He was, of course, to the small arrivals at Dean Close, an apparently formidable personality. " My first recollection of Dr. Flecker is of a huge person in a flying black gown and mortar board disappearing down the school corridor after I had said good-bye to my parents for the first time." It is this image which expresses something of a wider and more general effect. Many of the notes of gratitude which have been written about him praise him for his justice. But justice, so praised, always implies power. "The chief impression that he made on me," wrote a junior colleague, "an impression deepened by his complete mastery of a vast and highly-centralized organization—was that of Power; or rather of a conflict of Powers; an immensely strong will now driving, now curbing, a nature of intense emotions and of dynamic restlessness that might easily have become uncontrolled impatience. The tension and sense of urgency thus developed in himself was communicated to most of those who served on his staff. He could not endure incompetence or half-heartedness."

It is one example of this that he was said to have been able, at any moment, to take any class in any subject. But the subjects on which his own lessons seem to have been most admired and best remembered were history, mathematics and divinity—meaning by the last word the Greek Testament and the Book of Common Prayer. (They are indeed an admirable group.) His voice assisted him there. "No-one of my generation," wrote one Old Deacanian, "and I expect for several generations afterwards can forget the enthusiasm and intricate knowledge displayed in his Sunday morning lectures on the Prayer-Book. Here he was thoroughly at home and drilled us well in the historical and controversial aspects." (But for the young controversy is apt to be simplified. There is a story that in one history lesson Dr. Flecker asked one boy to describe the character of one of the Popes. The ardent student answered: "He was an evil man and greatly increased the power of the Papacy." The class broke into loud laughter. It was not very long before that such an answer would have been taken seriously both by master and class about almost any of the Popes. Flecker did know what history was, or the class would not have been amused.) The Collects, of course, were used, but also those less well-known parts of the Prayer-Book, the Prefaces. "No one", says one writer, "passing through Dean Close in the years of his Headmastership went away ignorant of these flowers of the English language." He did obviously love English; Donne and the Prefaces are

DEAN CLOSE SCHOOL

THE PLAYING FIELDS

the proof. It is, obviously, one of the most difficult clauses in which a Headmaster can have to instruct his charges. He must either become weak or seem hypocritical. So one would think. But the general testimony is that Flecker was neither. "Christianity," wrote one Decanian, "became part of the natural life of the school."

If so, it was because the tension in Flecker himself was at once real and resolved. The voice that controlled, instructed, and exhorted could also chat and exchange intimacies. It has been said that he was not one of those unwise masters who insisted on conversion. He did not attempt to use his authority unfairly. One of the Old Decanians has said as much: "He very wisely refrained from using his position to exercise what might have been construed as undue influence on us personally." Another's account may be quoted in full: "I had not been many terms at Dean Close before my life became all awry and the vision of my own happy home and that of the Fleckers began to fade. On returning to school after one Christmas holiday I found that three of my best friends had been expelled. It was a terrible shock. I could hardly believe it and could not understand it: but the fact that I had been associated with these three showed me how precarious was my own position. What did Dr. Flecker think of me now? If I saw him coming down the corridor I slipped out into the quad before he reached me. In the school he was always the Head: in the home he was the father. It was the Head with whom I now had to deal.

"At that time there was in the school a 'pi-squad.' I do not remember Dr. Flecker ever attending the meetings. They were run entirely by the boys themselves—then about twenty in number. Their keenness was amazing. I think they must have noticed my case and seen my misery. I had no friend, I did not want one. I gave up my music, and lost interest in my work. One Sunday night I attended Chapel as usual; the sermon was preached by the late Bishop of Sodor and Man.[1] His message gripped me

[1] Dr. J. Denton Thompson.

as I had never felt gripped before. After the service I tried to read my book, but failed. At last I could hold out no longer. I slipped upstairs to my cubicle and knelt down and had it all out with God.

"I could not keep this to myself. I was smitten at once with the desire to let Dr. Flecker know first even before I got pen and paper to write to my parents. Why? Because he was above all a friend. I knew enough of him to know that behind all the cloak of sternness and the arduous duties that caused him always to appear in a hurry, deep down there was his *love* for his boys. I had seen him in his home as well as in Chapel and at work, and I knew he too loved my Saviour. I went ever so quietly down stairs, and crept along the corridor to his study. There was a fear that he might still be the Head and be stern, or perhaps he would disbelieve me. I had not been to his study before except to receive a rebuke. But cost what it may he should be the *first* to know, and at once though it was almost nine p.m. and a late hour at which to disturb the lion in his den.

"I knocked quietly. Yes, he was there and I was bidden to enter. He looked at me—and I shall never forget that look all my life. It was not a look of anger nor curiosity, nor resentment. There was never that with him. It was a look of kindness from a heart of love. He may have seen that I was nervous, he asked me what I had come for. I told him that that very evening I had opened my heart and Jesus had entered in. He believed me at once. It seemed as though he had been expecting this. I never knew till then how closely he had been watching my movements and praying for me. He told me he had.

"That great man took me kindly by the hand and drawing me to the side of his chair he talked with me and then we knelt down and he prayed with me. Then we got up. The Head smiled and put his arm around me and took me to the door. Then he shook me warmly by the hand and wished me God's blessing on the future.

"I left Dean Close a year later, and we became the closest of friends."

It is, of course, clear that in spite of Dr. Flecker's own self-restraint, the atmosphere of the school was calculated to produce such a result on a young mind of that character. But this was the purpose of its foundation and the wish of many of the boys' parents. Dean Close was in no sense improperly using its advantages. A personal devotion to Our Lord, and a knowledge of the Rites of the Church was what it was there to encourage. It is clear from many letters that the encouragement was successful, and the success lasting. Part of that success was perhaps due to the infiltration of religion by laughter. Another incident may illustrate this: "Then I remember another incident in the schoolroom, a streaming wet Saturday afternoon which kept us all in. Dr. Flecker had just discovered Jacobs who was then quite new to us. He brought a volume along and read us a short story whilst both he and we rocked with laughter. He was a marvellous reader. The story was about some skipper who had to navigate the ship in his wife's clothes. I never saw him laugh again as he did for that reading of the story by Jacobs."

The athletic side of the school was not neglected. In one year Dean Close won the Gymnasium Shield for all England, against all the other schools in England. Of another year Mrs. Flecker has recorded a pleasing story of the Head of Cheltenham College who on the occasion of a cricket match between the second eleven of Cheltenham College and the first of Dean Close, came late in the afternoon to console with Dr. Flecker over the loss of the match (owing to the superiority of choice among numbers at the College) and arrived just as Dean Close won.

In 1906, on his silver wedding, when he had been there for twenty years, the Committee of Government presented to Mrs. Flecker and to him a tea and coffee service of handbeaten silver.

"By the Governing body of the Dean Close Memorial School, Cheltenham.

"In token of their high and grateful appreciation of the work done by him, not only in the development of the school, but also in the furtherance of the best interests, intellectual, spiritual, and moral of the pupils committed to his charge. August 1906."

There were other gifts from members of the Committee individually with kind messages.

Shortly after came a promising and tempting offer to take a West End Church in London. It appealed to him very much. But the Committee felt his attitude deeply. "If it were a bishopric that were offered you, we should have had to let you go—but to be an ordinary vicar of a parish such as any clergyman can be is quite different. Not everyone can run a school like this. We should never have bought that large field if we had had any idea that you would leave us. It seems almost a dishonourable thing for you to leave us." "If you consider it a question of honour," said the Headmaster, "I will stay."

Two or three anecdotes, contributed by old boys of the school or by Mrs. Flecker, may here be given.

"A rather backward School Certificate Maths. Class venturing down the dim paths of Algebra; the Doctor approaches the blackboard with the light of enthusiasm in his eye. Follows that characteristic gesture of the hand passed over the face and 'Now,' he says, 'Now we will do this really nicely.' Slowly and with admirable precision and neatness the progressive lines of orderly figures begin to stretch across the board. But as the chase grows more exciting, faster and faster flies the revealing chalk, more and more illegible become the mystic symbols, until with a shout of triumph the elusive X is tracked to her lair. The audience is limp and breathless with the unavailing effort to keep up. A wistful smile from our teacher shows sympathy with the non-mathematical mind and we start again."

"A young prefect—unduly young because a Great War was claiming all the elders of that generation—somewhat nervously enters the notorious Rooms 1 and 2 to take Prep. He reaches his desk. For a time quiet reigns, but all eyes are on him. He is unaware of the fact that above and behind his desk has been erected a masterpiece of indoor engineering composed of compass boxes, books, inkwells, and other noisy elements. According to plan the erection falls with a most satisfying crash. Hilarity is the order of the day. *Not* according to plan, the Doctor enters. He gives one look at the prefect, whose head is unbloody, but just a fraction bowed, one look at the room, and marches out without a word. That prefect never had any more palaver in prep."

"A leading man in Cheltenham came to Flecker one day in the early days of the school and said, ' My boy has just been expelled from his Public School—but only for want of discipline. Now you are a very small school, and could look after that fault better than a big school could. Will you take my boy; he is nearly seventeen.' This interview made the young Head think much. After all this was the son of a distinguished man. If he could make a success of him it would be a great help to Dean Close in its infancy—but if he could not? However, he decided to try the boy. He was a big fellow for his age— good at games—but soon showed that he did not mean to be mastered if he could help it. One evening after the boys had gone to bed Flecker said to his wife, ' I believe if I went up and gave that fellow a good thrashing before the other boys I should have no more trouble with him— he's not really a bad sort—but he needs to feel he is not master.' His wife was a bit nervous; this was an unusual experience. She said, ' Suppose he turns on you? ' Flecker laughed at the idea and went off. There was never any more trouble with this boy. He turned out well and made a success of his life. He had found someone at last who was not afraid of him. This success was widely known in Cheltenham at the time and gave Dean Close a good reputation. There was a sequel. His father came to Flecker again at the beginning of another term, and asked him to give his son another flogging. 'What for?' said the Head. The father began a story of what the boy had done in the holidays. 'Oh, no,' said the Head, 'I don't punish for what is done in the holidays. Besides, don't let his father be frightened of him.'"

In 1914 when war broke out, several masters left for the army, and Flecker had to add their classes to his own, besides carrying all the other responsibilities of anyone in such a position. He was only able to get women-assistants, and the larger schools had had their choice even of them. Those whom he did secure were the least effective. Mrs. Flecker has written: "This alone was a great trial to him. His natural politeness struggled with his disapproval of their incompetence and of the airs they assumed." His own younger son, who had been educated entirely at Dean Close was in Mesopotamia. But his younger daughter came to his help. She was then at the Royal Free Hospital, doing medical work and studying to become a doctor. She gave this up, and returned to Dean Close. She took over the whole of the chemistry teaching, with excellent results, and relieved her father in many other ways.

The war ended—more exactly, it was suspended—in 1918. Six years afterwards, Dr. Flecker retired from the Headmastership, in 1924. He had been pressed to stay until the Memorial Chapel—to the memory of one hundred and twenty old boys who had been killed—had been built. He had consented to this, but afterwards he was reluctantly determined to go. The final ceremonies took place on Saturday, 20th July and Sunday, 21st July, 1924. Saturday was the Speech Day. Flecker could see round him on that day, as so many do not, the testimonies to his success. There, where there had been but a small block of buildings, with one class-room, were all the new erections: the main school, the dining-hall, the senior house block with Prefect's studies, the sanatorium, the gymnasium, the baths, the science laboratories, the Memorial Chapel; there were the new playing field, the masters' houses, the houses for junior boys, the workshops and another fifteen acres of ground recently bought for future use. Instead of the dozen boys, of whom the majority had been brought there by himself, he and Mrs. Flecker entertained to dinner on the Friday evening, seventy old boys; two hundred and fifty boys of the moment dined also in the school. It was no small achievement.

On the Saturday a service was held in the chapel; Flecker himself read the lesson—the immortal proclamation by St. Paul of the Nature of Love. If—he read, knowing well what he read—if he had given all his goods to the poor, if he had given his body to be burned, and if he had not love, it was all of no avail. The remarkable voice sounded again in that high place, before the altar of that Love, among those he had desired to bring to that Love. He had sought it for himself—Love that does not envy, that is not puffed-up, that never thinks evil, that is always courteous, does not brag about itself, puts up with everything, is tender at heart, hopes, endures, believes. In all that respectable company, the great passionate definitions went on; "they heard, and were abashed." Yet this was the root of all; he had the courage to say so, and it became him. He was not, even then, "behaving himself unseemly".

At the Speech Day ceremony Flecker himself spoke, in the usual way, on the term's work. But when that part was ended, the greater part began. Sir Thomas Inskip, now Lord Caldecote, recently Solicitor General, and then President of the school, spoke; so did others of the Governors. They recounted the past; they expected, with hope and goodwill, a fortunate future. But mostly they nobly praised the real maker of the school. He had "achieved the impossible"; he—they knew it very well—was the true founder; on his foundation, all that was to come must be raised. From without came other voices; for example, the Chairman of the Headmasters' Conference, Dr. Alington (then Headmaster of Eton, now Dean of Durham) had written in gratitude.[1] Those who spoke, spoke also of Mrs. Flecker's work; they alluded, naturally in inadequate words, to that strange and lasting wonder of marriage, in which so many who have known it discover that those august definitions of Love come, to the immortal astonishment of those who endure them, to be true. They turned again to their main theme; it was this man who had done it—none else—and now he was leaving his work. And they too wisely praised him for, and in the name of, Love.

They presented gifts: a cheque for £5,000 from the Governors, a desk and a library chair and a cheque from the parents of the present boys (and a Chippendale china cabinet for Mrs. Flecker), a canteen of silver from the Old Boys; these were followed later by a hall clock from past and present members of the staff, and a set of silver salvers from the boys, on which was inscribed " *Monumentum et Pignus Amoris*". Flecker answered; he too spoke of the past, and of all the goodwill he had himself received. He claimed, and he had a right to claim, that the School, while remaining faithful to its intended principles, had been free from tyranny or bitterness. It had held all the freedom that there could be; it had looked forward always to the full freedom of the City of God.

On the next day, the Sunday, there was an early Communion Service. At the morning service Flecker preached— on the things that are " honest . . . just . . . pure . . . lovely . . . of good report,". "Think on these things"; these which are, for all darknesses of sin and misery, native to the mind, but must be held by effort and organized habit; these in which we hope and to which we return. He had tried to maintain and elucidate the vision; they told him he had done well.

[1] At a Headmasters' Conference held at Dean Close, he had said earlier: " Some of us have been given great schools to look after, Dr. Flecker has created this school."

The term had ended, and his scholastic career. Dean Close had begun. He had known the greatness of the work, and the toil—a little of the achievements. He had begun what was greater than he; none knew it better than he, or was humbler towards it.

V

THE FAMILY

ONE of the boys at the school, now a Lieutenant-Colonel of artillery, wrote of his arrival at the age of thirteen: "I was a nervous boy when I entered Dean Close, as the home-life had meant so much to me. Dr. Flecker must have discovered this, for almost at once I was made welcome in his house from time to time. In this way I came to understand that a Headmaster can have that fatherly love that means so much. There were many happy visits, and though Dr. Flecker was not able to spend long with his family, when he entered the drawing-room there was always a flutter of excitement and happiness while he stayed."

Flecker's son-in-law, also a Headmaster (of St. Lawrence College, Ramsgate, and Ipswich School), has also written a note which shows the relation between the house and the school:

"I first met my father-in-law at a 'Dons and Beaks' Conference at Cheltenham in the year 1908. At that time some of the Undergraduates at Oxford and Cambridge were running camps for public school boys. Doctor Flecker was interested in these, and I spoke in their defence. At the end of the session, he carried me off, in his genial way, to lunch, our common interest being heightened in that we were both headmasters of Evangelical schools. In the interval before lunch, he handed me over for entertainment to his elder daughter (Mrs. Flecker having had a slight accident), an ill-advised step for one who valued the integrity of the home. From that moment began a growing intimacy with the Flecker family, which—all unsuspecting—opened its door to, perhaps, a rather persistent stranger.

"What impressed me, from the first, was the enormous vitality of the home-life, and the wonderful way in which it was carried on, without interference by the School and its many distractions. The home-life was a very precious and carefully guarded thing. At the same time, in a wonderful way, the home atmosphere expanded into the School, so that one felt that, in a sense, the School was an extension of the family. There was, I suppose, no public school in the country where the school was in more intimate relation with the Headmaster and his wife. The instinct of fatherhood and motherhood was so strong in the pair that it overflowed family bounds and included boys and servants in the family relationship.

"The School had begun as a very small community which was, in fact, a little family, and the family atmosphere had never been lost."

Who then were the members of this family? The Doctor himself and Mrs. Flecker; the eldest son, James Elroy, whose birth has been noted and of whom something more may be said presently; and the other children. James Elroy was three years old when the second child was born, a daughter Claire, whose arrival her elder brother resented. Claire was extremely delicate, and it was chiefly on her behalf that a house for the holidays was built at Southbourne. She was followed, in four years, by another daughter, Joyce (now married to a Headmaster in the Midlands), and by a son, Oswald, (now Headmaster of Christ's Hospital, Horsham).

It is, however, clear from the records that all four children were intelligent and even brilliant creatures. Claire grew up to be so lovely that her mother has said: "She heard so many remarks on her beauty that I tried to make her look as plain as I could; it was very difficult." She went to Cheltenham Ladies' College, and from there took her B.A. degree at London University. After her marriage in July 1911, to the Rev. E. C. Sherwood, who wrote the note quoted above, she took a London Diploma in Theology, and lectured on it to ordinands in a small college started by her husband after he resigned from his

Headmastership and took a cure of souls near Cambridge. She also wrote two books (*The Starting Place of Prayer*, 1929; *The Road*, 1935); something from them will be quoted in the next chapter. There were three children. But her health was often not good, and she died at Staines while still in her forties.

Something should be said of the relationship between Flecker and his more widely-known son. It is clear to anyone who reads Dr. Hodgson's life of James Elroy that it was a perfectly normal relationship. Indeed, it seems to have retained something more of affection than such relationships sometimes do. Dr. Hodgson's book obviously exhibits how completely intolerable James Elroy could sometimes be; she is driven to stress the smallest courtesies in his letters as signs of deep gratitude. No doubt there was gratitude on his side as there was certainly generosity on his father's. His manners were not noticeably worse than the manners of the young to their parents generally are. But they were, at times, pretty bad. This is perhaps a desirable dispensation, for often nothing except bad manners is capable of piercing the mail of habitude which the older generation has put on. But that hardly excuses the bad style—especially when, as in this case, the parents seem to have made every effort to understand and assist.

There were, of course, other difficulties. "He had," his mother has written, "a great dislike of being one of a group. He disliked playing in concerted music, or in being one of a party to listen to me reading. He liked a solo part always." He had a marked tendency to feel that, if he wanted anything, from books to fame, he ought to have it at once. If he could get it himself, he would; if not, some one else must get it for him. Yet he must not be made to feel dependent; they must think of it as a privilege. He had a sincere gratitude, but his gratitude must not feel under an obligation. Dr. Hodgson writes:

"Two things only occasioned any real strain between him and his parents. The first was comparatively unimportant—his unwillingness, at all times of his life, to keep any sort of rational account of the money he spent. For a man of moderate resources, he was wont to spend more than he could afford, mainly on books and pictures to which he took a fancy, and which he was convinced he ' could not do without'. The other was more serious: it centred round his friendships, and turned mainly on more or less religious considerations. His sisters and brother were younger than he, and his friends were not always what his parents desired to have brought into the home circle."

There was in the young Flecker all his life a serious attachment to his father and to his home. It began early enough; they were companions on their walks. The son went to Dean Close School, where he learnt those religious principles on which it was conducted. He evidently took them in. "He is", a friend wrote, "a real Christian of the Evangelical school." This remained so till he went to Uppingham when his opinions began to change. It is a common and in a sense proper thing that this should happen. The Faith cannot be accepted second-hand; somehow or somewhere the individual answer must be made. Occasionally this happens without any preliminary revolt; generally it does not. It did not in the case of James Elroy. On 17th October, 1901, he wrote a letter to his mother from which the following extracts are taken:

"Take prayer meetings first: take the——prayer meeting. I attended it once right through a term. I now analyse my reasons for attending it. My reason was, I found, not to obtain help; nor did I go there because I enjoyed praising God. No: I went there simply because I had a vague idea I would go to heaven if I attended prayer meetings, and please you at the same time.

"Again, what were the results of the said attendance? I heard very similar exhortations every time, as I have heard in every single thing of the sort, conversion, etc. Believe in Christ—nobody ever took the trouble to explain what is meant by this faith—for that, we must look to the miracle read in this Sunday's lesson, which gives the three stages of

Christian faith: *credo Christum, credo Christo, credo in Christo* (I believe Christ, I believe in Christ, I believe on Christ).[1]

"Well, the result of this continual firing of texts into my ears, which the firers did not understand any more than I did, resulted in good resolutions. Which same lasted one, two or three days as the case may be, and during that time I used to add a minute to my prayers, think a little over what I read in the evening, perhaps even go so far as to try and mean what I said, or realise what I heard in Church on Sundays, with a sneaking conceit that there were not three other people in Church who were trying to do the same.

"What a farce indeed Church is! I do not write this down without thought. Every Sunday I grow more and more convinced. Say it was *un peu outré* to go to Church: would not the benches be crowded! Some go because they must, others because they want to go to heaven, others because it would be remarked if they didn't, others from some vague sense of fitness, others to study fashionable dress. What hypocrisy could be greater than this! Then words are read out, old and inadequate—in beautiful English true, but we do not go to Church to study English —and they absolutely *must* lose all meaning for most people through their parrot-like repetition."

This distrust of the purely emotional (very proper to him as a poet) had led him to underrate the place of works in the Evangelical idea. But there is nothing to show that he ever had a theological mind, or that he ever understood the place that theology holds in the tradition of Christendom. At seventeen, or almost seventeen, this is natural enough. But at an older age it obviously invalidates any opinions on the Church. On the other hand he wished very strongly to discuss the primary question of whether Christianity was true, and he could not find any apologetics adequate to his need. Evangelicalism has, on the whole,

---

[1] This seems an inadequate translation. The stages are surely: I believe Christ, I believe in Christ, within Christ I believe. The progress is from formal belief to real belief, and then to unitive belief. (See also p. 76).

tended to start from some kind of spiritual experience, or at least the conscious lack of it. But James Elroy was at the moment demanding rational proof. "At this time," a friend wrote during his early Oxford period, " he became violently anti-Christian." But it seems to have been a swaying opposition. Buddhism, of course, came in; Buddhism always does come in.[1] He wrote: " Though I would rather be a ritualist than an Evangelical, I would rather be a Buddhist than both." But in his complaint about the lack of intellectual distinction in the Evangelical school there was some justice.

Among those minds he did allow to be notable, his father was one. " Of all the Evangelicals I know," he wrote, " Father, Gray and the Bishop of Durham (Dr. Moule) are the only ones whose brains command the slightest respect." He adds that " the collective brain-power " of " the twenty odd Evangelical undergraduates I know . . . would not suffice to run a tuck-shop." He complained in another letter that his family would " admit Kensit and turn out Huxley." This, after all, even had it been true, would hardly have been surprising. But in fact his father, as fathers must, pointed out the inevitable commonplaces which underlie the whole question, and are no less rational for being commonplace. He wrote pointing out that " theology is an abstruse science," and that our Lord had laid down that " the doctrine shall be revealed to those who are prepared to do the will. So that if a man—if you should take the Beatitudes as the law of life and determinedly obey them, the question of dogma might wait. . . . There is a stiff book of Ward's on *Naturalism and Agnosticism* worth reading."

The son's letters continue for some time more or less in the same strain. He says he dislikes " the gabble of the Prayer Book "; he has " a wondering contempt " for the metaphysicians who have come in his way; he wonders " that any sane man can believe in Christianity "—and

[1] I have forgotten who was the author of the charming saying: " I always think Christianity and Buddhism are so much the same—especially Buddhism."

so on and so on. These are phrases from casual and intimate letters, and must be taken so. They are natural enough, but they are, of course, of no serious value, and they do not even begin (oddly enough, considering his undoubted ability) to raise any intellectual objection. He retained a strong feeling for his father's companionship; in 1904 he wrote to him that he wanted to come to Chamonix where the family were " (i) to have a companion (ii) to have you as a companion (iii) to be *en famille*, and I want to discuss prospects."

There is no necessity here to go into further details of those prospects and of his life; they can be found either in Dr. Hodgson's biography or in the introduction to the *Collected Poems*. He went on relying on his family and they went on being that adequate reliance. They helped him financially; they responded to his needs, as far as was at all possible. This, no doubt, was proper; but then they did what was proper. At one time he proposed to his father to come to Dean Close as an assistant master.

" The more I consider matters, the more sure I am that the very best thing for me would be a place at Dean Close. The question is of course, will you take me? I badly want to clear myself of the stigma of being an obstinate pig, unamiable, insubordinate and tactless; I should like to show you that I am perfectly able to work hard, to keep to my work, to get on smoothly with the other masters, to be unobtrusive in my views and manners. . . . Will you try me on probation for the end of this term? There is perhaps some boy trying to matriculate or some small form that I could take.

" I don't want to be given clever boys to teach. I shall be quite content with a low form. I am willing to give up all notions of going for a holiday if you will try me till the end of this term. All the difference that I should ask between myself and the other masters is rather less work and in consequence rather less salary."

This would obviously have been quite impossible. " Is it not a good thing, sir," said Boswell to Johnson, "that a son should live with his father?" "No, sir," Johnson answered; "if it were we should see it succeed more often than we do." And a modern poet has written: "It is a father's office to be scorned." The stress is on the word "office"; it is—or may be—part of his business, his vocation, as a father. He need not take it too solemnly. In 1906 James Elroy wrote indignantly that his father took "no interest in anything except that your son should have an honourable and comfortable position. I don't think it is being offensive to say this. I suppose that it is natural that it should be so. I have sent you a poem now and then, you never sent a word of criticism. I naturally might not accept what you say, but the ideas of anyone with any fondnses for literature are valuable, especially when it is one's father. I still feel myself wronged. Much love to both of you."

He was wrong about the offensiveness. But many fathers will recognize the dilemma in which Dr. Flecker was thrust. Criticism was demanded, but it is likely that it would have been resented. The father continued to fulfil his office. When the young poet's illness began to develop, he offered him a house and an income in England. But the son did not wish to be dependent. He wrote in 1912: "I am so disheartened. It is my tragedy. . . . No one will do anything for me." But in another letter he saw through this: "One gets a sort of mania of persecution . . . a form of excessive self-pity, which is quite physical and passes away when one is well."

"By 1913," says Dr. Hodgson, "owing to various causes . . . he had moved away from the vehemence of his Oxford days." He had begun to learn more of the other great Churches of Christendom. But he was still writing in one letter: "My ideas about [Christianity] would probably irritate you badly," and in another: "Why not ask me what sort of Christianity interests me?" This is to trail one's coat before one's father, in order that one may be equally annoyed whether he does or does not jump on it. His mother added a note on the last quotation: "His parents naturally rejoiced in his return to the Christian faith, although the colour of his views was not discussed in spite of this expression of his wishes." There is generally a point at which the parent cannot any more bring himself to jump on the trailed coat.

In his last days at Davos " he did his best to reproduce the atmosphere of his old nursery at Dean Close." He wrote to his mother: " How touched I am at the constant way in which you write to me. It's you who really love me, dear mother," and again: " I yearn for the affection of my family, and above all to see you." It was in this more tender and courteous mood that he also wrote in 1914: " It will please you to know that I intend to take Communion this Xmas. Please just mention your pleasure in your next letter. I have not been suddenly converted or anything like that. It is partly that B., though a very nice man, was rather feeble and has gone, and this extremely nice old saint from China has turned up: partly that I feel the attraction of the English church service and Bible, and the Englishness of it all too keenly to turn to foreign creeds however much attractive.

" But I must admit and want you to know that the general wobbliness of the English church is a great nuisance to me, and that I am bound to be, as a poet, a thorough ritualist and detest anything like Welsh Revivals. Sorry to muddle Joyce—please send my Teacher's Prayer Book—and some Greek Testament or other.

" I wish people did not think it necessary to honour God by packing the Bible into one volume, with double columns and bad print, with ugly black leather—and all divided into stupid little verses. How grand it would be to have the New Testament at least, in a fine volume, printed like a real book, and *not* the Revised Version."

Dr. Hodgson says of this: " Flecker bought a Tauchnitz copy of the Authorised Version of the New Testament, and had it bound in singularly beautiful blue ' half calf.' Failing to get a facsimile for his mother, he sent her, for a birthday present, his own copy at Christmas. The Authorised Version of the Bible and the Greek Testament, together with the Book of Common Prayer, were increasingly prized by him in his Switzerland days, and were always within his reach. At last, he was glad that his wife should read the daily Evening Office aloud to him; and thus, in his pain and growing weariness, the words of the Gelasian Collect of the fifth century brought to him the priceless remembrance and assurance of 'that peace which the world cannot give.'"

He wrote to his father, early in that December:

"God bless you, dear Father. Your disappointing son is getting rapidly better, and once he is well enough to write a reasonable amount, which, pray God, will be in the spring, will probably support myself six months every year from literature alone—if not more. Do you realize your son is thought by Gosse, Yeats, Gilbert Murray, and also, thank God, by some editors, to be far the greatest poet of his day, barring Yeats? Is it not worth a year's illness to be great? I think so. Do write joyfully.

Roy."

By the end of the month he was very ill, and the chaplain was himself too ill to bring him Communion at Christmas. At his wife's request another priest, also himself a dying man, brought it to him on 3rd January. He died in the afternoon of the same day, Sunday. That evening the telegram announcing his death reached Dean Close, while his father was preaching a New Year sermon at Christ Church, Cheltenham.

The body was brought home to Cheltenham in a British destroyer and buried in the cemetery there. A memorial tablet was put up, first over the temporary Chapel door, then to the wall of the new Dean Close War Memorial Chapel. It reads:

In loving memory of their son,

H. E. FLECKER,

Poet,

His sorrowing parents have placed this tablet.
And thou shalt see the gleaming Worlds
As men see dew upon the grass.

Of the grave Dr. Hodgson writes: "A plain grey granite curb surrounds his turfed grave, and for the grey granite cross, engraved with his name and the dates, his wife chose the last six words of his *Hexameters*, prefixing them with the Invocation:

"O Lord, restore his realm to the dreamer."

Upon the cross hangs a wreath of bay, perpetually renewed. In the grass of the grave grow an Alexandrian Laurel and an Olearia Hastii, the gift of his mother, which are the nearest approach to *Oak and Olive* which cemetery rules and the English climate permit.

He had written, in an early letter from Uppingham, that if he should gain any success, "You yourself, my dear father, are the prime cause of everything." Even earlier he had dedicated an MS. book of verse to his mother with the following lines:

> Come with me to the forest-glade,
>   And list to the lilt of a tune;
> Come, but come in the evening shade,
>   In "the cold clear light of the moon."
>   Tho' the tune be too rough
>   For the Muses nine
>   And the melody all untrue
>   Yet strange to say
>   O Mother Mine
>   I offer the tune to you.

There had been, at the end, a certain more mature recurrence of this awareness. He was reaching the point—it was not an easy one to gain—where, in Alice Meynell's phrase, his emotions would come to birth already justified.

> There is
> One great Society alone on earth,
> The noble living and the noble dead.

VI

THE WAY

WHAT then was the idea—say, rather, the power—in which Flecker and so many of his contemporaries lived? the thing which provoked some and contented others? the austere beauty which ruled the lives of those believers? It is perhaps less popular to-day, and even less understood, than the other tradition of rites and sacraments, but it has always been a moving element in Christendom, and we shall do well to try and understand it.

It would be, of course, improper and false to divide the two traditions—called, colloquially, the Evangelical and the Catholic. A passionate devotion to the Person of our Lord is common to both. Wesley was a sacramentalist and Pusey evangelical. But on the whole it is possible to discern in the history of the Church militant here on earth these two stresses, of which often at any particular time and place one is more definitely felt than the other. In the eighteenth century in England it had in general been the Evangelical tradition which had been the more vital, and this lasted on into the nineteenth and is still active to-day.

The characteristic of this mode of Christianity was—speaking with all possible modification—not only a devotion to our Lord, but a specific belief that this could be realised consciously and its results consciously experienced. It believed that some experience of this kind was all but a necessary preliminary to the Christian life. This great sense of conversion was its root. It did not, at its best, demand any such intense and profound experience as an absolute necessity, though its less wise teachers seemed sometimes to talk so. But it did tend to measure everything and interpret everything in the light of that experience or that belief.

Its dangers were (i) a disproportionate undervaluing of the present world—an attitude which has given rise to the colloquial sense of the word " Puritan " (ii) a casualness about the instituted Christian " means of grace "— the sacramental life and the ordained ministry. Both these dangers Flecker seems to have avoided with natural good sense and remarkable skill. He had grown up in a tradition against which, unlike his son, he had never revolted. Like the great doctors of Alexandria, he grew at once in the graces of this world and the grace of another; he breathed heaven in with the common air. He had to make no violent retrogression in order to find Christ; he had not to agonize as Augustine and others of the " twice-born " did. It was a fortunate and blessed fate. " It is a good thing," Mr. Belloc has written, " to have loved one woman from youth, and it is a good thing not to have to return to the Faith." Both these elements of good fortune were his. It was probably this naturalness of love and religion which enabled him to accept natural blessings—and to practise them. He had, that is, nothing of the " Puritan " attitude towards intelligence and beauty.

His early admiration of Donne would be a proof of the first, perhaps of the second. The present writer is aware that he may seem to stress this too much. But it cannot too clearly be grasped how unusual, for a young Evangelical, training for the ministry and for teaching, such a knowledge of Donne was in the eighties. It was " a stiff book " of Ward's that he recommended to his son, who said nothing more about it. James Elroy was much better at poetry than at argument, but even he admitted that his father had one of the best brains he knew; it is an honourable admission. Flecker never shared any distrust of the holy intellect. A sermon preached at Staines on Armistice Day, 1936, is worth quoting on this point. He was already intensely aware of the growing national danger, and he had been speaking of re-armament. " There was," he had said, " perhaps something to be said in favour of having no armaments at all." But he went on to urge that there was nothing to be said in favour of having inefficient armament—" enough to provoke, not enough to repel. I am not convinced that our re-armament will be carried out as effectively as it ought to be. No one can read our military history without feeling grave misgivings as to the civil and military leadership of our armies. . . . The story is, to say the least, a very disquieting one. The fact is that military leadership demands superb brains and supreme self-abnegation, and we as a nation rather despise brains. In addition we need attention to the minutest details. . . . I am sure that there are no more honourable leaders in any state than in ours. But honourable men are not always very clever, and our statesmen are pitted against men who seem to be too clever for them. No doubt the demands on them have of late years been increased tremendously partly owing to the swift transmission of news. And the situation is on all hands acknowledged to be grave. It is not the fault of statesmen that they are not so able as men say of the eighteenth century. It is a national defect. We are not a clever people; we distrust brains. No other country would have invented such a slogan as " Too clever by half." The test of a nation's greatness is its capability of producing great men. I think England shows a great capacity just now of producing able little men."

The Staines paper, reporting this sermon, had a subheading: " Brains despised." It was this sense of a lack of intellectual attention in the English that seemed to him, on that Armistice Sunday, to be responsible for the procession of the dead in the last war, and of all those who lived hurt and maimed lives because of that war; and now as the danger rose again—" if that procession were to pass us, what could we say? We could but tell them it was all a terrible blunder. Let them go back to their graves and rest." As for the living—they would continue to despise brains, and to reap the too terrible results of despising brains.

This does not, of course, mean that he thought brains the only way to the Kingdom of God. No one was less likely than he to forget that kind of faith which is the one thing necessary—which feeds hope and introduces charity; which (multiplied twelve-fold) becomes the gates of the Divine City, and which is the only sufficient cause of all earthly affection. He had a profound love for and admiration of the simple believer—" Christ's silly sheep." But if certain sheep had been called to intelligence, he conceived it their duty to fulfil their vocation. And (along with the whole Christian Church) he believed man to be a rational animal, and that he should behave rationally. It was (as he said in the sermon quoted above) man's duty to be political; it was the business of everyone to be concerned with what went on in the " High Court of Parliament." He was a Liberal; he believed in Liberty. He believed also, in secular as in religious affairs, that Liberty meant choice and decision; and that any man who to the best of his power does not choose has thereby abdicated his manhood, and is like the beasts that perish. Or, more dreadfully, grows into his own " perishing," as the Athanasian creed foretells.

At the same time, the intellect outside grace can never be the same as the intellect inside grace; if only because all the premises available to it are changed. Whether or not there is in any one soul an experience of " conversion " —that is, of an entire change of values, it is certain that that change of values must take place. It may come violently and catastrophically; it may come gently and continuously. It may be welcomed; it may be resisted. But when the intellect becomes aware of it or assents to it, then the intellect is conditioned by it. To say it conditions is not to say it deforms or limits, except indeed as all premises must limit. The intellect working in a world in which the Incarnation has happened is not obviously in the same position as the intellect working in a world in which the Incarnation has not happened. But it has to learn to operate on the new premises. " A certain definite training of the intellect was demanded," wrote Claire Flecker, " for the manifestation of God is also conditioned by that wherein He is manifested. . . . I fail to see with what reasonableness we look for God to be manifest through an element or species we have taken no trouble to understand. This setting of our intellects to learn is one of the most beneficial pieces of discipline."

Her attitude had been derived from her home and her father. " I cannot," she wrote in *The Road*, " tell how greatly I am in debt to a home where family prayers were as natural as food or to the earnest sincerity of him who led them." The serious value of her book is a tribute to her training, and to the intellectual freedom of her home. Her father had not discouraged questions, or she would hardly have given him " with my love " a personal copy of her book;[1] which begins by saying that her generation " questions everything hitherto held fundamental," and concedes them every right so to question " God, Christ, marriage, parenthood, public schools, conventional morality, authority, the Church." She seems to have been able, both in her father's home and her own, to follow her own paths, to examine her own assumptions, to inquire into her own problems, to discover her own beliefs, without having to exhibit it quite as spectacularly as her brother.

Devotion and the intellect were not the only elements in the general life of Flecker's household. It is a mark of the distance between his day and our own that it is difficult for us to speak about Beauty—just so, with its capital letter and all. All those abstract nouns have suffered somewhat. One can hardly read a serious book of late Victorian days without coming across them—Beauty, Truth, Goodness, and so on. They were perhaps overdone; perhaps the war ruined them for us. But it is of some interest to remark that it was not quite so that Flecker saw it. He himself had always had a sense of beauty, whether in literature, art or nature; but he did not think it common. In some notes for a Rotary Club address at Staines, he has written: " Great contempt of Beauty in nineteenth century? Subtle effect. Together with contempt

[1] *The Starting Place of Prayer*—Preface.

of Beauty enormous growth of absorption in Games."
There is perhaps more to be said for this than at first
appears. Beauty, like everything else, is easier to talk
about than to discover or explore. Personified, it becomes
of doubtful value. But Flecker was not, it seems, given to
muddling up talk and action: like Patmore he was not
" given to mistaking words for things." This is a great
temptation to all schoolmasters. They are compelled by
their duty to talk; they have to go on talking; and by the
end———? In his case, it was not so.

He was very greatly aware, as the years passed and
especially the post-war years, of the sense of despair which
prevailed in many places. Chesterton had written of it
even before the war, and the answer which King Alfred
gave to the Danish king and earls in the *Ballad of the White
Horse* was, inevitably, Flecker's:

> On you is fallen the shadow
> And not upon the Name.

He read Wells; he read Bertrand Russell; he quoted the
noble and dark passage in which Russell speaks of " the
firm foundations of unyielding despair," upon which alone
can the soul firmly build. But though the same Rotary
notes show that he quoted it with respect, he answered
it with something more than disagreement. One note
runs: " To despair of England—Traitorous." But if it
was high treachery to despair of one's country, it was an
even worse betrayal to despair of Man. And he felt that
that treachery was affecting very many of the common
people. " The essence of life is not travel through space
but travel through time, and the wayfaring man is uncertain
of the purpose and end of his journey." In a sermon
broadcast from Staines on 6th November, 1932, he said that
" there are thousands who live that ' unexamined life '
which Huxley said was unthinkable for a human being."
Flecker and Huxley would have disagreed on many things,
but both of them possessed that sense of responsibility
which is one of the marks of the adult mind. Flecker has

a note that his mind compared to Russell's is "a newt to Newton." But he shared with both of them that desire to live "an examined life" which is one of the capacities and duties of Man.

He had been serious about it in his youth; he was serious about it in his age. He had tried to encourage the boys at Cheltenham towards it, and he brought the same effort and effectiveness to his congregation at Staines. More will be said about his work there in the next chapter. It may however be noted here that his Evangelical fervour did not lead him to ignore the traditional sacraments of the Church. His register of visiting notes on occasion that a baby here and there has not been baptized. But he did not confuse the personality of the priest with the power of the Spirit. "How I wish the clergy would believe how delightful it is to be in Church sometimes when they are not speaking!" he noted. All that made up the personality must be given, but all the personality—all his personality, and all others—could not do more than lead to "the examined life." That must be the free choice of the soul.

It was within that examined life that he and his people discovered what the noble agnosticism of Huxley did not discover—that other life which is the communicated life of Christ. To discover that is at once the climax and the transfiguration of responsibility. Responsibility remains; the great doctors and mystics of the Church do not, for all their surrender and loss of self, lose that. They only fulfil it, but that they now do. "I had as many battles after my conversion as before," said Wesley, "but then I was sometimes beaten; now I was always conqueror." So with this other servant of the Faith. It is impossible to ignore the cloud of witness to his effectiveness; it is—given the Faith—impossible to doubt whence that effectiveness arose.

He did not, it seems, lose any of his normal and natural characteristics. He still read widely—Shaw and Chesterton and other writers, contemporary with him, were in his library. One friend writes that the last time he saw him he was chuckling at a joke. He attended to "the decent beauty" of the services in the church. He urged—as in the same Rotary Club address—the duty of attention to political affairs; to neglect this again was something like treachery to England. But all these things were touched—it is a poor word; say; in the strictest sense of the word, enlivened, by the sheer existence of our Lord. That other life infiltrated everywhere. It was this which controlled and directed him. *Credo in Christum*—he had believed in the Faith; *credo Christo*—he had felt a personal faith in Christ; *credo in Christo*—he was joined to Christ and (living so in Christ) he believed.

VII

STAINES

HE had left Dean Close; he was sixty-four. He must go where he could work. He must (incidentally) also have a place where he could house his thousands of books. Eventually the Fleckers moved back to London—to Croydon where a house was found with a billiard room which could be turned into a library, and was. It could also be used for meetings, and was. In the enthusiasm and energy of these different surroundings he made a beginning on the new life by mowing the lawn, only to bring on a severe attack of neuritis. One cannot suddenly begin to be physically laborious at sixty-four without paying for it.

But if this had to be stopped, the cessation only gave him more time for occupations more habitual and perhaps more dear to him. There were old friends—some connected with members of his former congregation at Lee—and new friends. There were clergy needing help—as, for instance, the invalid Vicar of St. Stephen's, Wandsworth. Mrs. Flecker has noted that the only difficulty here was his great dislike of Sunday travelling. This was in the true Evangelical tradition, but apparently Flecker allowed a Dominical command to override it. He "pulled the ass out of the pit"; he went to Wandsworth. A more considerable work which he took up was that of a speaker on behalf of the British and Foreign Bible Society. He did this voluntarily and without payment because of his passionate admiration of their work. He was always a missionary at heart; it was why he had gone to Dean Close. He could not himself go farther now, but he could vicariously. He travelled wherever necessary in England.

He went especially to the North, always with crowded meetings.

In all this he was sufficiently happy. The pain which had been caused to him by his leaving Dean Close passed away; the continuous activity on behalf of the divine thing encouraged and satisfied him. And more perhaps than to some, the divine thing itself allowed him a reward. It not only filled him with itself, communicating joy by its own most blessed nature, but it filled his life with the delicate loves of friends and with the gratitude of disciples. Disciples is a permissible word; it was from him they learnt it first, and afterwards went on to learn the same thing directly from his Lord. "To be with him," wrote one, "was to live elsewhere, to live a different life. We knew, there, the one Necessity."

"The examined life," "the one Necessity," whatever words can or may be used mean always the same. He continued in that activity for three years and it continued to flourish round him. But he dreamed of more arduous labours, of a narrower home; he brooded over the possibility of a parish in the slums. He was not, it seems, offered one. Instead, he was offered the care of a church and congregation at Staines. The church was a lovely modern building, created by Sir Edward Clarke. It was dedicated to St. Peter. Sir Edward knew Flecker personally and in 1927 offered him the charge.

He was inclined to accept; there was, however, a small but important difficulty—there was no Vicarage, nor could a house be found. The previous Vicar had been a bachelor and had lived in rooms. All search for something suitable failed. The possibility of work at Staines receded. Flecker always insisted that he must live among his people. The Vicarage in another living offered him lay at the top of a hill, near the church, and among the reasonably well-to-do. At the bottom of the hill, half a mile distant, lay the poorer houses. "Find me a house among *them*," Flecker said, "and I will come." He must be, he knew, a Christian priest; on the duties of his vocation he could not compromise, and one of them was to be the neighbour of those to whom also he was to be a light and a guide. A light at a distance, a guide whose voice has to be discovered, were not what he believed his vocation to mean.

Staines had almost been forgotten when Sir Edward wrote again. There was a house on the other side of the church from Sir Edward's own residence; it was to be sold. It was small; it was inconvenient; but it might serve. Would the Fleckers come and look at it? They did. Flecker looked at his wife. Sir Edward looked at her, saying: "Could you make it into a home?" She answered her husband: "If you will give half your books to Oswald, and all the big furniture and carpets, we will manage." Oswald was the second son, who had just been made Headmaster of Berkhamsted School, and had a large Tudor house to furnish.

They arranged it so. But the house at best was inconvenient, especially from Mrs. Flecker's point of view. The Croydon house was large; this was small. It had no larder, and the original dining-room was the only possible room in which the books could be kept. A new dining-room had to be built at once. The old one was turned into a study; three thousand books were put into it, together with the desk and chair given him by the parents of the Dean Close boys.

Flecker was then sixty-seven. It was the autumn of 1927. He had before him fourteen years of work, till he died at last at eighty-one. The whole of that time could be summed up in a phrase from one of Sir Edward Clarke's letters: "I would not change my Vicar for any other in England." He had some reason to say so, for (as was recorded in the *Life* of Sir Edward Clarke) there grew up a great friendship between the two men. "In Flecker," the *Life* records, "thanks to the strong bonds of common religious outlook and intellectual endowment he found an intimate friend and a very, very pleasant companion. Such perplexities as did occur he was able to study with the one on whose wide reading and intellectual equipment he could rely." After Sir Edward's death Lady Clarke wrote to Flecker: "I want first to thank you for your beautiful letter and then for a gem of a sermon at the eleven o'clock service. It was, to my mind, a masterpiece: I loved every word of it as I feel sure every one in the church did. So much more difficult to say what is in your mind in a few simple words. I am sure you cannot realize what you were to my beloved husband, ever since you first came to St. Peter's. He loved you, I know, and was always so grateful for your visits. I saw the light come into his face when you entered the room. What I should have done without you I do not know. I thank God for sending me such a true friend."

This relation with Sir Edward was typical of Flecker's relation with his other parishioners. It is not always the easiest thing for a Headmaster to relinquish his office and assume the office of parish priest. There is apt to linger in him something of that necessary monarchical attitude— something in the voice, in the glance. The sovereignty of a headmaster and of a priest are different; there is, no doubt, authority in each, but authority itself has to take on the style, the behaviour, proper to its circumstances. Flecker had been a Headmaster for many years. It is true he had sincerely wished to encourage individuality. But it is one thing to encourage individuality among the young, and quite another to encounter it among the grown-up. The desire to encounter and experience real authority may be in the grown-ups even more than in the young; it is very widespread, if not (as it well may be) universal. But where a child submits, an adult freely submits; the difference is not negligible. Authority does not, among the adult, do away with freedom; freedom indeed lies precisely in the choice of submission. Authority, if it is to avoid tyranny, must be continually invoked freshly that it may act freshly. " I have not called you servants," said our Lord, " but friends "; and added in a paradox not always observed: " Ye are my friends if ye do whatsoever I command you." Is entire submission a characteristic of friendship? One must, of course, consider his nature who spoke. Friendship with Incarnate God must differ from all other kinds. Yet it is true that in certain states a real and free friendship thrives in such a surrender, and individuality leaps, distinct and bountiful, from what might seem, to the uninstructed or inexperienced, the very denial of individuality.

That great tradition of conversion, of bringing souls to God, lay behind—say, within—the whole of Flecker's life and career. He had, it seems, been permitted to be untouched by the sinister temptation which too often accompanies it. He had never thought that to bring souls to God meant to bring them to himself. His patience, his tolerance (to use a noble word nobly) of the charming, but tiresome and adolescent, intellectual crudities of James Elroy are the best proof. He might be hurt—that was inevitable; he might occasionally be annoyed—that was natural. But he had always remained sympathetic, and (as it were) *there*. He was expected by his son, of course, as so many fathers are, to be at once entirely one with his son and yet quite other than his son. (This, let it be added, is also true of many fathers; they desire entire "replicas of themselves" which are yet to be quite different from themselves.) It could not be done—not even to please James Elroy. But what could be done, he had done. So, with all those others. He had meant to bring them to God; that is, to themselves in God; not to him or even to themselves in him. He freed them while he bound them; at the height of his influence on them he refused it, and bade them refuse it too; they must be beyond even that. So passing beyond it in their new profession, they found it restored to them, in friendship, in authority, in wisdom, in humour, in charity.

This had been true, it is clear, of a number of the boys at Dean Close. It was true now of his parishioners at Staines. This indeed is the only way in which that pastoral office can be properly exercised. A priest must always be a priest, but both he and his people must know how to deal with that priesthood. It must be always there, yet it must never be a cause of offence: "woe to him who offendeth one of these little ones!" It must be always itself, yet never go beyond itself. This was Flecker's immediate duty; this, certainly, he fulfilled. He proceeded to be at once a teacher and a friend. The parish was wide-spread; part of it lay one and a half to two miles away, and presently this part began to grow. It was, as they say, " developed." Flecker called at every new home not only with the proper pastoral greeting but with offers of any immediately needed help. This was in addition to his other visiting, on which he set great stress. He went out on it every day. The records of his visits are full of all sorts of jottings to keep details in his mind: " W. G.—adenoids just removed "; " The A's.—Wesleyans: would like a visit "; " Mrs. H.—send fruit "; " Mrs. K.—go again soon "; " Mrs. F.—grapes "; " Mr. D.—built a greenhouse "; " Miss O.—*must* get to see her "; " J. O.—wishes to leave all property to me, I to invest for grandchildren "; " the R's.—children don't come to S.S. for want of clothes "; " Mr. R.—ill; ordered eggs "; " Mrs. C.—boy wants a job "; " Mrs. W.—quarrel with husband "; " S.—cricket club "; " Mrs. M.—roof practically finished "; " Mr. P.—years ago in choir; his resignation never acknowledged; long talk " (does one hear the talk!); " Mrs. S.—gave her 10/- "; " Mr. S.— ' I'm Protestant ' "; " Mrs. S.—will come to Confirmation if Mrs. L. comes. Mrs. L. thinks she is just as good as some as has been confirmed "; " T. B.—has been a drunkard; suggestion of prayer ' gave him a headache ' "; " Mr. R.—go again when the lilies bloom."

And so throughout. These annotations leave those of a more pastoral kind unquoted; the many about baptism, confirmation, Communion, coming to church, prayer. Every now and then there is a note of warning, of one kind or another: " No. 71—evil dog! "; " No. 62—mother too plausible." Flecker had no intention of being bitten in any sense; he firmly believed in a certain serpentine wisdom. But in general the whole register is full of sympathy, encouragement and serious priestly love. There are, no doubt, thousands who have worked, and work, so. In thousands of parishes such visitings are, as it were, the frontier between the Church and the world. Flecker was one of a great number; to say so is not to diminish him but to understand them. What seems to have distinguished him particularly is that he had not only love but the courtesies and the style of love; love not only in purpose but in action; love behaving itself seemly—that is, as love should and only love can. His children and near relatives looked to him for the baptism of their own children and for the introduction to sacramental life.

In a very few cases there is a note saying: " Better not call." But in general he was met by friendship as free and courteous as he offered. It was particularly noticeable, for example, that brides at whose weddings he had officiated wrote often to him on the anniversaries of the weddings, even reminding him of words he had used in his addresses. Family life is not always a subject upon which the clergy are at their best. It is true that Flecker's own marriage had been peculiarly fortunate, but it is not necessary to suppose that others are not. He seems to have had a power of saying things effectively; he was not given to rhetoric, but neither did he fall into interminable series of cliches. He had a sense of life happening, and it was that life happening with which he was supremely concerned.

There were, of course, the inevitable special cares of the parish priest. The church had to be re-roofed at a cost of £500, and this had to be raised, Flecker being unwilling to have it charged as a debt against the church funds. The church was not endowed, and the Vicar had an extreme dislike of asking for money. He realized quite acutely the financial state of many of his poorer parishioners, and he was more than doubtful (bearing that in mind) whether he ought to allow himself certain conveniences; thus, though he kept a car for the use of his wife who was unable to walk far, he would never make use of it for visiting, and felt it (apart from that sole reason) slightly unchristian to possess one at all while so many lacked so much. He was, however, sometimes compelled to make appeals for help for the church. He rather reluctantly decided on one occasion to do what had been done at some other churches, and on St. Peter's day to sit in the church to receive gifts for it. The result was astonishing, and the custom was regularly adopted. The gifts were brought, certainly primarily for that Church of St. Peter, but it was not Flecker's fault if they were not also felt by the bringers to be offerings to the whole Church " militant here in earth."

The same thing was true about the cheques which came from his richer parishioners. Here however Flecker was willing, if not to spoil the Egyptians, at least to be grateful to the Indian. The prince and cricketer Ranjitsinhji was a near neighbour. He became very friendly with the Vicar. He sent a cheque for the church, and answered to an expression of gratitude: " But how then could I spend money better? " He even, knowing Flecker's reputation for scholarship, proposed that his nephew should be coached by him for matriculation, but Flecker felt he had to refuse; this work would have threatened to encroach on the parish work. He was willing to do anything he could of the kind unofficially—and did, for several youths—but he would not take on other responsibility; the people of his cure must come first.

The prince's household also became very friendly. An aunt even came sometimes to the church (" Christianity," she said, " was only another form of Hinduism "), and she and others of the princesses paid calls at the Vicarage. The Prime Minister, a Parsee and a very widely-read man, became even more intimate than the prince. The grounds of the house were lent for a church fête, which the prince attended; though tea at the royal table was interrupted, it is said, first by a telephone call from the Prince of Wales (afterwards Edward VIII) and then by a summons from the Majesty of England himself. The prince had to leave at this, but left orders that all should go on as if he were there in person.

The great problem which in these years confronted Flecker was the arrangement of the parish. As it grew, he became acutely conscious of its need for more spiritual help. He wanted a mission-church in the more distant part, largely for the sake of the children. It was a long way for them to come to church and Sunday School, and dangerous, what with the unfenced river and the roads becoming weekly more crowded with Sunday cars. He worked hard to get this church. The then Bishop of London (Dr. Winnington Ingram) was always appreciative of Flecker and sympathetic to him personally; he referred to Staines as one of his " happy parishes," visited the house, and invited Flecker to preach in St. Paul's Cathedral. The Evangelical and Catholic traditions of one Gospel moved harmoniously together in those two priests. But on the matter of the parish he said he could do nothing, unless Flecker were willing to surrender that part; then a church could be built and a priest appointed. It was a great regret to both the Bishop and Flecker, but eventually it had to be done. The division was made. But many of those on the farther side of the dividing line refused to recognize it. They continued to come to St. Peter's; they claimed still to belong untechnically to the parish; they made it clear that they still regarded Flecker as their parochial father-in-God. As time went on, and he grew older, the parishioners insisted on the appointment of a curate, but this was to ease and not to oust the Vicar.

There were also, of course, the other parish activities. There was the choir. It was a good male choir, of about forty, but it did not like being criticized and it did like to decide what it would do. On one occasion, soon after he came to Staines, it went into a small revolt. In front of the church is a large space of green sward, having some fine elm trees; it is divided from the tow path and the river only by a very low fence. Flecker determined to hold open air services there on Sunday evenings in the summer; they were to consist mostly of hymn-singing, in order to attract the attention of those in boats or on the path. He explained his plan and made arrangements. It was a lovely evening; chairs had been put out, and a portable organ; the evening service ended. Mrs. Flecker waited. Presently the Vicar came. " It's all off," he said; " the choir say they won't come outside. If anyone wants a service, here's the church; let them come in." It is, of course, a tenable point of view, but it was a great disappointment to the Vicar.

He was much concerned about the boys of the choir, and did all he could—not without some success—to make them feel their part in the service. Occasionally he felt them almost too much so; thus he was disturbed by the fact that at the monthly Choral Communions, communicants on their way to the altar had to pass between two rows of watchful and critical boys. He also thought that the boys should not be compelled to attend two full services on Sundays; he would much have preferred they should have had opportunity to come to the Sunday School. But even he could not abolish that custom. It is a notable tribute to him that when he himself spoke to the Sunday School children in church once a month, a number of the choir boys did in fact come to that service as well as to the other two. In the ordinary services the choir had before his time been left during the sermon to sit in their usual seats; they were left with the impression that the sermon did not concern them, and they occupied themselves, discreetly or indiscreetly, as they chose and could. Flecker altered this. He had front seats in the nave reserved for them; he caused them to walk down to them in procession during the hymn before the sermon and to return during the following hymn. It made them part of the congregation, whether they liked it or not. It is to be remarked that such a practice may have a good effect on the preacher (though in Flecker's case the reminder was not needed); it presents him with a direct audience who must be immediately interested. But the introduction of this practice makes it the greater tribute to him that so many should have cared to hear him again in the Sunday School.

He carried his concern with children beyond both his family and his official relations. Thus he took the trouble to arrange for the pupils of all the private schools in the neighbourhood to come to St. Peter's on the high, and too much neglected, Feast of the Ascension of our Lord. Many of them only saw the inside of a church on that day; but then it was filled, boys on one side and girls on the other. The Vicar made it his particular business to see that both service and sermon were proper for them.

There were also more secular activities. He was for some time Vice-Chairman of the local branch of the Middlesex Education Board, where his past experience made him extremely helpful. He worked very hard in order to get a scheme for the physical betterment of children above fourteen accepted. In this he strongly believed the tradition of the Church which proclaims grace " both for the body and the soul," but here he was concerned not only with Christians but with all. He called it the " difference between just keeping alive and being fit " (but it may be noted that this applied also to his whole doctrine of the spiritual life; to be just alive in grace was a poor thing; to be " in condition," to live by it in all the energies, to be wholly strong—this was the desirable end). There is a note written by himself on his efforts, and as so little remains of such things, it may be given here:

" In the spring of 1937 being much concerned by the thoroughness in which the Physical Fitness of boys and girls above school age was being promoted and the comparative neglect of it in our country I drew up a scheme which I thought we might try out in Staines. I submitted it first to the late Mr. Percy Low, Chairman of Staines Council, and to Mr. Sowrey, well-known as a most generous supporter of any movement for the well-being of youth. Encouraged by them I asked some sixteen people who by their position might be expected to be interested, to meet and talk things over. Very few replied or came to the meeting but the scheme was well received by those who did take the trouble to consider it, and on the strength of that I sent the scheme up to the National Advisory Council on Physical Fitness. The Secretary replied, ' I think you are exactly on the right lines, in fact we are ourselves exploring the possibility of adopting nationally a plan such as you have in mind. But,' he went on, ' I wonder whether you would like to hold your hand for the moment before taking any steps in Staines.'

" Well, of course I waited, but when six weeks had elapsed I thought that would be ' a moment ' in the eyes of Whitehall and I wrote again only to receive this reply: ' We are hoping very much to do something of this kind nationally but it is unlikely that we shall be able to go far with it before the autumn, and I think it a pity if you were to find later that anything you had planned locally could not be brought within a national scheme.'

" Well, this was rather damping. However in the summer a new Act was passed altering the whole situation: it authorized Local Authorities to provide or maintain or to assist Voluntary Organisations to provide or maintain playing fields, community centres, clubs, gymnasia or other facilities for social or physical training not only for young people but for people of any age.

" It was suggested that grants might be applied for by October 1st. So, greatly daring, I wrote to our Urban Town Council in September, asking them if they were intending to avail themselves of the Act.

" The reply I received was, ' the whole question had been before the Council some time ago and the recommendation of its appropriate Committee was adopted last evening.' I took that to be a polite way of saying ' Mind your own business,' and I minded it. And I do not know what, if anything, has been done, or is being done in Staines. You may very well say, ' What is the use of flogging a dead horse.' I admit the reproof—the reasons which have actuated me are these.

" A fortnight ago there appeared in the *Times* a leader urging the adoption of a scheme which was almost identical with that which I had brought forward.

" Secondly, this is the fourth time in the last eight days in which I have been called upon to speak to young people of Staines.

" Thirdly the percentage of rejections of applications to enter has fallen from 60 per cent. in 1936 to 47.7 per cent. in 1937 and to 37 per cent. in 1938."

He was also for years on certain London committees and on the Staines Hospital Committee, and made a point of visiting the hospital regularly—as priest or as simple visitor. He had a great power of extempore prayer. It is on record that one tubercular patient was known to be dying when Flecker, calling on him at his home, prayed with him. The patient began and continued to recover. Certainly there may have been various causes for this; certainly also there may have been but that one cause— that at least was promised (under conditions) to the Church.

But the Church, as he saw it, was in schism. He could not do much, but he thought he could do something, and he was always unwilling to think and not to act. He proposed and took steps to form a " Council of the Churches." Apart, of course, from the Roman Catholics, all the Christian bodies in Staines, from the Church of England to the Salvation Army, were represented. It took notice of anything proposed for the betterment of Staines, and did its best to bring the Christian idea to bear on all civic life. The Congregational minister was the Secretary; Flecker was Chairman. Such bodies are more commonly established to-day; without involving controversy on doctrine, they have been much used in non-doctrinal affairs. It may be noted here that after Flecker's death, the Roman Catholic priest wrote of him: " His unfailing kindness was an example to us all "; the Congregational minister: " He was so big and so simple, and both qualities so in harmony that it was easy to miss that secret "; the Rural Dean: " To be with him and talk about things was a constant delight." All the tributes tend to stress not only his sympathy but his intelligence. One of the Secretaries of the Church Council wrote: " As Secretary to the Church Council I studied very carefully the Laws and Resolutions relating thereto, and Dr. Flecker made use of this knowledge, but I discovered that he also knew these things and his questions were placed only as a check to his statements and a kindly way of demonstrating to those present that his secretary knew his job."

Another tribute to the same power but to a different use of it may be also conveniently given here. He was great friends with an architect living in the neighbourhood, a Nonconformist; they had a common interest in ecclesiology. This friend wrote of one conversation: "It was I think the last time we met in his study, a room which now holds for me most precious and sacred associations. I went to consult him about the significance of the phrase! "the Word of God" and its varying interpretation in the Bible. From his knowledge of the Scriptures and especially in the Greek, our conversation ranged from the utterances of the prophets to the mystical vision in St. John's Gospel of the Divine Logos. . . . And, as a contrast, I have a most vivid recollection of a casual meeting in the street, shortly before his death when he was on his way to the Library to change a book. We walked together for a while—he was, I could see, not very well. When we parted he was chuckling over 'a ruthless rhyme' which had tickled his fancy, and which he wanted me to share."

He continued in this work steadily, with that extra note of felicity it sometimes pleases Almighty God to bestow. That sense of felicity ranged from what it is possible to call a celestial joy to what is generally called "a sense of humour." "A sense of humour" is in the contemporary world often expected to bear burdens it was never meant to bear and to gain results it was never meant to gain. It is admired almost as much as sanctity in other ages and no one is complete without it. Much, as a proper capacity of man, we may allow it; yet it is but "a secondary grace." It will no more ease a broken heart than heal a broken leg. Flecker possessed it, and kept it in its place. There are many testimonies to his quick apprehension of good jests and anecdotes; there is nothing to show that he ever over-rated it. It may be that a sense of proportion is one of the rewards of "the examined life." In any case, the sense of humour is best kept in proportion by a sense of felicity; this again is dependent on humility; and that again on love. So ordering his own decencies of the spirit, he continued always to practise love.

It would be too much to say when the second outbreak of war came, that his felicity was not wounded. But the infelicities of this world do not, at bottom, disturb the felicity of that other; in some sense, it is necessary to believe that of our sacred Lord himself. Somehow, somewhere, that felicity sustained him; since in the end what sustains all is precisely felicity. And in the clients and companions of our Lord? certainly in his clients and companions. The darkened point of joy remains joy. In a funeral sermon Flecker on his own behalf quoted St. Paul: " Finally I am persuaded that neither death nor life, nor angels, nor principalities nor powers, nor things present nor things to come, nor height, nor depth, nor any other creature shall be able to separate us from the love of God which is in Christ Jesus our Lord." He spoke the mere truth; he was so persuaded. That high persuasion had remained valid for him through the first war; it remained, even more victoriously, through his part of the second. The older he grew, the more he displayed what one of his friends called " the contagion of a triumphant spirit." It was effective through all his sadness and anxiety about the war, through the bombing of Staines and the casualties among his people, and (where so often it fails) through the occasional weaknesses of his own old age.

His health had remained surprisingly good. He noted in his record of visits: " On my seventy-first birthday I was able without undue fatigue to do ten and a quarter hours real work. Thank God! " But certain slight disabilities crept on him. He had always loved singing— from those early days when he had first gone to the house of his wife's people—but now he became slightly deaf and could not always catch the pitch of the singing in church. Holidays helped him though he did not waste time even then. He disliked going to hotels, and for some time preferred to make arrangements to go to some other Vicarage and take the services. Presently a parishioner offered him each August a house at Worthing, and there he and his wife used to go in the summer; but he made a habit of spending the morning reading on the pier. He very greatly desired to preserve his intellectual activity, and to be aware of the contemporary world. On 1st August, 1931 his wife and he celebrated their golden wedding;

in 1941 their diamond wedding. On each occasion they tried to keep it secret. On the first they were at their son's house at Christ's Hospital, Horsham, but letters and telegrams arrived there, and when they returned home they found the dining-room table covered with gifts of flowers. In 1941 they celebrated the family festival privately at home, with the two living children, two sons-in-law, a daughter-in-law, and some of the eight grandchildren. Two maids, who had been with them for fifty-four years were included in the gathering. A service drawn up by Oswald Flecker was held in the church; it was taken by him and by his two brothers-in-law, but Flecker himself was asked to pronounce the benediction. Church and State —the Bishop of Kensington and the Chairman of the Staines Urban Council, and others—sent congratulations. So public, in spite of Flecker's wish, did the day at last become, that he was compelled to write a letter of thanks to the local paper. He spoke of his experience as that of most of the clergy; "it justifies," he wrote, "an aged parson in continuing his work with thankfulness and sincere humility." The sublime definition of gratitude given in Milton may be properly applied both to him and his people.

> The grateful mind
> By owing owes not, but still pats, at once
> Indebted and discharged.

There was everywhere a proper exchange of love.

He was then eighty-one. He had had in 1938 an attack of pneumonia, but he had entirely recovered. In 1941 he had had an accident and scalded himself; he had to be in bed for some days, and (perhaps for the first time in his life) suffered severe physical pain. His wife has noted that he never seemed quite so well after. But once he was up, he seemed, except to her, much as usual. His hair was still dark, and his voice clear and strong. He was still vigorous. On Sunday, 24th August, 1941, while his curate was away, he had taken all the services, including the early Communion Service. He spent the next two days in many visits, and showed no signs of distress, physical or mental. In the evening of the 26th August, three friends came to supper, one of many years' standing, Mr. Johnson. After supper Flecker said to his wife: "I will keep Johnson here in the dining-room, and you take the two ladies into the study; they'll like to hear the nine o'clock news." It was so done; he and his friend sat down in the armchairs on either side the fire-place, talking. There, suddenly, smiling as he spoke, he died. Mr. Johnson had gone hastily to tell Mrs. Flecker her husband was ill, but before she could reach him he had passed. The doctor, when he came, said: "He must have been very happy when he died," and added: "He died a young man." In some sense that was true, but not in any easy pretence of youth. He had had no nostalgia for childhood, nor had he ever wished to remain mentally or spiritually adolescent. He had in all ways desired wisdom; so, best. The Bishop of Kensington (now Bishop of Southwark), preaching at the funeral, praised him for four things—he was a gentleman, a scholar, a friend, a priest. Each great vocation supported and strengthened the others: courtesy, accuracy, love, faith. But perhaps the word which best unites them all is that used by his son in preaching in the church on the unveiling of the memorial tablet. He spoke of the Divine Compassion. It is a very great word; it is perhaps the most awful, absolute, and significant of all the names of God in relation to men. The very war in the midst of which Flecker died was, beyond all its other characteristics—if we are indeed to call it anything beyond a political war for Danzig and Poland—a war of and for compassion. The word is the most intense name for the unity of men and women. It was in that unity that Flecker had lived; it was for that unity that his son praised him. He ended: "It was fitting that he should close his career of service as Vicar of St. Peter's, for he followed very literally those charges given to the great apostle by the lakeside after the Resurrection. 'Feed my lambs,' look after the young people—'Tend my sheep,' give general guidance to the flock of Christ, young and old alike. 'Feed my sheep,' supply the needs of the adult and mature, look after them. I know that many of you in this congregation did not look in vain to your late Vicar for guidance and care and spiritual sustenance and that you found in him that real sympathy which he learned every day by walking humbly with his God. He loved much."

The tablet itself, put up by the parishioners in the body of the church, reads:

In affectionate memory of

Dr. W. H. FLECKER

Beloved Vicar of this church

1927–1941

formerly Headmaster of Dean Close School
Cheltenham.

Rest eternal grant unto him, O Lord!
And let light perpetual shine upon him.

www.ingramcontent.com/pod-product-compliance
Lightning Source LLC
LaVergne TN
LVHW011428080426
835512LV00005B/326